DECLINE AND FALL

■ ■ ■ ■ ■ ■ ■

DECLINE AND FALL

Europe's Slow-Motion Suicide

Bruce Thornton

ENCOUNTER BOOKS ❖ *New York · London*

First edition published in 2007 by Encounter Books,
an activity of Encounter for Culture and Education, Inc.,
a nonprofit, tax exempt corporation.

Encounter Books website address: www.encounterbooks.com
Manufactured in the United States and printed on acid-free paper.
The paper used in this publication meets the minimum requirements of
ANSI/NISO Z39.48-1992 (R 1997) (Permanence of Paper).

FIRST EDITION

LIBRARY OF CONGRESS CATALOGING-IN-PUBLICATION DATA
Library of Congress Cataloging-in-Publication Data
Thornton, Bruce S.
Decline and fall : Europe's slow-motion suicide/Bruce Thornton.
p.   cm.
Includes bibliographical references and index.
ISBN-13: 978-1-59403-206-6 (hardcover : alk. paper)
ISBN-10: 1-59403-206-8 (hardcover : alk. paper)
1. Europe—Civilization—1945–
2. National characteristics, European.   I. Title.
D1055.T56   2008
940.56'1—dc22
2007032307

10 9 8 7 6 5 4 3 2 1

CONTENTS

■ ■ ■ ■ ■ ■

ONE

■■■■■■

THE ROAD TO EUTOPIA

WHAT IS EUROPE?

WHAT IS THE Europe of this book? Most simply, Europe comprises the twenty-seven countries of the European Union, with a single currency, a European Parliament, a European Court, a population of nearly half a billion, and a nine-trillion-dollar economy. Europe also includes those countries, like Switzerland and Norway, not formally part of the E.U. but culturally and politically similar, and others, like Croatia, Romania, and Bulgaria, eager to join. But Europe is more than the sum of its nations and languages and histories. "Europe is not a natural unity," the historian Christopher Dawson wrote, but rather "the result of a long process of historical evolution and spiritual development." It is a "medley of races," and European man represents "a social rather than a racial unity."[1] Europe is an idea, then, a set of values and beliefs, a certain way of looking at the world that defines the West in general.

Yet in the last few centuries there have arisen variations and developments of Western values and ideals that have increasingly come to define Europe and its vision of itself as a superior cultural and political order, one that can avoid the injustices and failures of the past and harness more justly and efficiently the burgeoning forces of globalization and technology and the "global consciousness" both are creating. Nor are these ideals and values confined to the geographical and political reality of contemporary Europe and the nations of the E.U. These same values and beliefs, in fact, are held by many in the United States, and represent a model that some Americans urge us to adopt, and others counsel us to resist.

The following pages are concerned with those ideas, values, and beliefs that constitute this European model, not just with the individual nations and peoples that make up Europe, though of course they will figure in the discussion insofar as they act on those beliefs and create institutions and policies that embody them. By keeping this focus in mind, we can avoid simplistic contrasts between a monolithic "Europe" and an equally monolithic "America." Many Americans, liberals generally, approve of the European model as something to emulate. Partly this reflects the place Europe has traditionally held in the imagination of some Americans. Like the Yankee ingénues in a Henry James novel, they have admired the Old World of sophistication, culture, and civilization that contrasts with the New World of crude, go-getting, frontier brashness. But these days this admiration more fundamentally reflects the belief that Europe provides a more humane and sophisticated set of social and political values.

In the presidential election of 2004, for example, Democratic candidate Senator John Kerry, who speaks French and spent childhood vacations in France, was touted as the candidate who, sharing the European distrust of force and preference for the management of crises through transnational institutions, could be more effective in relating to our European allies. In the words of French writer Bernard-Henri Lévy, Kerry is "a European at heart."[2] Thus as president, we were told, Senator Kerry could undo the damage done by the unilateralist, "Euroskeptic" George Bush. Bush's critics identified him as that most American—and despised—of cultural icons, a "cowboy" who, it was erroneously reported, had never even traveled to Europe.

In domestic policy as well, some Americans look to Europe for guidance on issues such as homosexuality, affirmative action, and the death penalty—indeed, in some recent Supreme Court decisions, justices have cited the European Charter of Fundamental Rights and rulings of the European Court of Human Rights in support of their decisions. Many also tout the European *dolce vita* lifestyle as a more humane and fulfilling way to live compared to workaholic, money-grubbing Americans. *New York Times* columnist Paul Krugman, for example, believes Americans have a lot to learn from the French about family values—an opinion Claire Berlinski calls "laughable" given that the French are creating fewer and fewer families, and almost 15,000 elderly French in 2003 died during a heat wave, their bodies chilled in warehouses while their children vacationed on the Riviera.[3] On many other issues, Demo-crats and liberals in general align with the same values and ideals that underlie the European model, as conservative Jonah Goldberg indicated when he complained that President Bill Clinton "thinks like a European."[4] As Timothy Garton Ash put it, "'Blue' [Democrat] America often turns out to be a European shade of pink. On several of the key social issues, American Democrats seem to be closer to Europeans than they are to Republicans."[5]

But just as many in America admire the European paradigm, many Europeans look to America as a model of economic and social order and foreign policy, and disagree with the drive toward a European unity defined in contrast to the United States. On these issues, one European nation sometimes opposes another, and within each nation are groups that disagree over various issues.

We often hear, for example, that Europeans are universally opposed to the death penalty. Italian president Carlo Ciampi claims that opposition to capital punishment is the "most eloquent signal affirming a European identity." The existence of capital punishment in America is one of the most frequently cited examples of how benighted Americans are in comparison to the more humane and civilized Europeans, who see capital punishment as "simply barbaric," in the words of one-time French minister of justice Robert Badinter.[6]

Yet among the European non-elite, opinions on capital punishment are often more similar to Americans' than are the views of the academic, political, and media elites with whom our own reporters and intellectuals tend to interact. When California governor Arnold Schwarzenegger refused to stop the execution of a convicted multiple murderer and founder of a vicious street gang, the city council of his hometown of Graz in Austria voted to remove his name from a municipal stadium—even though one poll showed that 70 percent of Graz' citizens opposed the move.[7] And in the E.U. states from Central and Eastern Europe, support for the death penalty remains high among citizens and politicians alike. In the Czech Republic, Poland, and Slovakia a majority of citizens support the death penalty, while both Poland's president and Hungary's former Prime Minister have called for its restoration.[8]

Or consider the European disdain for vulgar American popular culture, as reflected in the French government's restrictions on American movies via its Ministry of Culture, or in the anti-free-trade restrictions on "cultural products" in E.U. commercial treaties, or in French theater director Ariane Mnouchkine's famous description of EuroDisney as a "cultural Chernobyl."[9] Yet not just movies, but American popular music, clothing styles and brands, companies, food, and in some places even American holidays like Halloween and Valentine's Day have become part of European culture.[10] In 2005, the most popular movie in France was *Star Wars: Episode 3*. The all-time biggest hit in France is still *Titanic*. American popular culture permeates the taste of the

French, from the several hundred McDonald's and Starbuck's franchises to the popularity of Britney Spears, the person most googled by the French in 2004.[11] American high culture, too, attracts many Europeans, from the several thousand English-language books translated into European languages, to museum shows, like the 2004 Museum of Modern Art show in Berlin, which attracted a million visitors.

Perhaps the greatest division between the European mass and elite concerns the supposed evolution beyond nationalism into the supranational "Europe" of the E.U. This disdain for the nation may run no deeper than the bureaucrats in Brussels. According to the European Values Study, 90 percent of Europeans surveyed identified with their city, province, or country, while only three percent identified with Europe. What Tony Judt calls the "chronic absence of interest [in the E.U.] on the part of the European public" is reflected in voting patterns: between 1979 and 2004 voter participation in elections for members to the European Parliament fell an average of 20 percentage points, and the difference between the number of those participating in European Parliament elections and those voting in national elections ranged from 20 percentage points to a high of 43 in Sweden, a dismal level of participation duplicated in the new member states from Eastern Europe.[12] Well-educated, sophisticated E.U. functionaries and cosmopolitan intellectuals who benefit from the E.U.'s increased opportunities for supranational work, leisure, entertainment, and travel may believe that Europe has entered a "postmodern" world beyond the parochial loyalties of the nation and the dangers of patriotism, but the vast majority of Europeans who can not take advantage of those opportunities still find their identities within the borders of their own nations.[13] As Tony Blankley concludes, "The continuing attraction of nationalism is perhaps why voting in European parliamentary elections is so low, and why there is so much public resistance to a European Union Constitution." [14]

Clearly, attitudes within Europe about America, political issues, and cultural values are more various and complex than the simplistic America vs. Europe conflict suggests.

As well as conflicts between masses and elites within individual countries, there are important disputes between European nations over issues we sometimes think define Europe in general. Everyone knows that Europe is less religious and more secular than America—during the debate in 2003 over mentioning Christianity in the Preamble to the European Constitution, a French diplomat said flatly, "We don't like God."[15] Religion is indeed on the wane in Western Europe—church attendance averages less than five percent— yet many other European countries are still quite religious. Poland, for example, ruffled European Union feathers by taking the lead in trying to get the E.U. constitution to acknowledge Europe's Christian roots (the attempt failed). More recently, at the European Parliament in Strasbourg, Poles displayed an anti-abortion exhibit that linked abortion to Nazi concentration camps. A Polish European Parliament member has said, "We want to see Europe based on a Christian ethic," something no Republican in a supposedly evangelical-dominated United States would dare to say publicly.[16]

It is in foreign policy, however, that the dispute over which paradigm to follow, that of America or the European Union, has been most intense—a division to which ex-Secretary of Defense Donald Rumsfeld gave memorable expression when he spoke of "Old Europe" and "New Europe." Rumsfeld's comment was made during the acrimonious and divisive disagreement among European nations over the war to remove Saddam Hussein. France and Germany, of course, fiercely opposed the war, their leaders doing everything in their power to subvert a UN Security Council resolution in support of overthrowing Hussein. On the same day in

October 2002 that the U.S. Congress voted approval of the war in Iraq, the Norwegian Nobel Prize committee awarded pacifist Bush critic Jimmy Carter the Peace Prize. The committee chairman frankly admitted that the award was meant to protest a warmongering George Bush. And in February and March 2003, huge anti-war rallies filled the streets of European capitals.

Yet many Europeans supported the war against Hussein. In January 2003, eight European nations wrote a letter of solidarity with the United States' intention to remove Hussein, and soon after, ten Eastern European countries did likewise, causing French president Jacques Chirac to sniff that these nations' behavior was "not well-brought up."[17] Even in France, a few intellectuals and politicians spoke out in favor of removing Hussein, including Bernard Kouchner, founder of Médecins Sans Frontières, and philosophers André Glucksmann and Bernard-Henri Lévy.[18] In February 2003, twenty top French business leaders lobbied Chirac to end his opposition to the American-led War.[19]

Indeed, many European nations have contributed to the American-led wars in Afghanistan and Iraq. In the former, NATO forces are increasingly involved not just in providing security but also in actively fighting the Taliban remnants. Even France and Germany, bitter opponents of the war in Iraq, have been quietly helpful. German intelligence allegedly passed on Hussein's defense plans to the U.S. a month before the invasion, something the German government now denies. Before the U.S. invasion of Iraq, Hussein's foreign minister passed on intelligence to the CIA, using the French intelligence agency as a go-between. England, of course, has stood by the United States most steadfastly in Iraq. But many other European countries, including Poland, are still involved in that conflict. When sovereignty was restored to the Iraqis in 2004, sixteen of twenty-four NATO countries had forces in Iraq— a support subject, of course, to the vagaries of domestic politics, as shown by Spain's withdrawal after the Madrid train-bombings, Italy's withdrawal after Romano Prodi's election, and continuing anti-war sentiment in England. As Robert Kagan famously put it, Europeans are from Venus and Americans are from Mars, particularly the Europe of the European Union and its ideal vision; but clearly some Europeans are from Mars, just as some Americans are from Venus.[20]

Despite these complications and reservations, however, there nonetheless remains a comprehensive vision of political and social order consciously touted by many European nations and embodied in the activities and ideals of the European Union. This is the "EUtopia" that offers itself as a model superior to "American conditions," as ex-German Chancellor Gerhard Schroeder put it, using a code term that signifies everything negative and threatening about America.[21] Indeed, this EUtopia is frequently defined specifically in opposition to the cultural, social, and political orders of the United States.

This increasingly stark and acrimonious division between Europe and America is sometimes lamented as something new, a decline laid at the feet of President Bush, the alleged unilateralist "cowboy" whose lack of diplomatic sophistication has alienated our one-time friendly allies. Such a charge, however, ignores Europe's long tradition of suspecting American power and influence, particularly after the United States became a superpower and eclipsed European nations like England, France, and Germany that once swayed the world. Even during the unity forced by the Cold War, and the halcyon nineties after the fall of the Soviet Empire ended that conflict, disagreements and clashes have roiled America's relationship with various European nations, particularly France. The European preference for government solutions to social and economic problems has long distinguished Europe from the United States and its reliance on individuals and the market: "Nobody in Europe," English historian A. J. P. Taylor said in 1945, "believes in the American way of life—that is, free enterprise."[22] From the Suez Crisis of 1956 to the uproar over the deployment of Pershing missiles in 1983, which sparked a protest by two million Europeans, the interests of the United States and Europe have frequently conflicted.

Despite these disagreements, the continuing Soviet nuclear threat forced Western Europe to cultivate close ties to the United States in order to enjoy American guarantees of European security. Yet even during the Cold War, American economic power caused discomfort for many in Europe. In 1964, French political scientist Maurice Duverger wrote that "there is only one immediate danger for Europe, and that is American civilization," a fear seconded in J.-J. Servan-Schreiber's 1967 essay "The American Challenge."[23] Once the Soviet Union imploded and that threat disappeared, Europe began to find more concrete ways to assert its global prestige and independence from an America that had become what French foreign minister Hubert Védrine, in 1999, called a "hyperpower." That America was as much or more a rival as an ally of the French was made clear in 1996—also during the Clinton administration, before the advent of the "cowboy" Bush —when French President François Mitterrand said, "France does not know it, but we are at war with America. Yes, a permanent war; a vital war; an economic war; a war without death."[24]

Nations, obviously, pursue their own political and economic interests, and for many European nations, these interests will conflict with those of the United States no matter which party holds the presidency. Yet the "postmodern" EUtopian ideal is supposed to transcend such parochial national interests and realist power politics and move, in Robert Kagan's words, "beyond power into a self-contained world of laws and rules and transnational negotiation and cooperation."[25] This disconnect between the professed ideal and the actual behavior of European nations calls into question the viability of the EUtopian "postnational" vision, a theme to which we will return.

THE EUROPEAN PARADISE

We should start by defining the ideal that the European Union is supposed to embody and that many in the United States believe its own citizens should embrace. Indeed, as presented by its champions, the European social and political order will make the twenty-first century the "New European Century," in the words of one enthusiast, for it will be the solution to mankind's perennial ills, and a recipe for creating heaven on earth.[26] One of the more enthusiastic champions of the E.U. vision, Jeremy Rifkin, believes that a "bold new experiment in living" has arisen in Europe, and that the Europeans are "leading the way into the new era." This "European Dream," as Rifkin calls it, "emphasizes community relationships over individual autonomy, cultural diversity over assimilation, quality of life over the accumulation of wealth, sustainable development over unlimited material growth, deep play over unrelenting toil, universal human rights and the rights of nature over property rights, and global cooperation over the unilateral exercise of power." And unlike a worn-out American dream mired in the past, this dream "represents humanity's best aspirations for a better tomorrow," an estimation seconded more soberly by the professional historian Tony Judt, who finishes his history of Europe since World War II with the claim that Europeans are "now uniquely placed to offer the world some modest advice on how to avoid repeating their own mistakes," and that "the twenty-first century might yet belong to Europe."[27]

The content of this European Dream is a laundry list of the utopian Enlightenment ideals of the last three centuries. In terms of foreign relations, as summarized by Kalypso Nicolaides of Oxford University, the E.U., the institutional mechanism for managing and expanding the European Dream, endorses "supranational constraints on unilateral policies and the progressive development of community norms" in order to create a global, interstate Kantian community of "autonomous republics committed to relating to each other through the rule of law." This "security community" will favor "civilian forms of influence and action" over military ones, and strive to create "tolerance between states" and to "move beyond the relationships of dominance and exploitation with the rest of the world." Its guiding principles will be "integration, prevention, mediation, and persuasion," which bespeak a faith in rational discussion and negotiation rather than in the old realist reliance on military power to maintain global order by deterring and punishing violators of the peace.[28]

This vision can be further fleshed out with a letter published by French philosopher Jacques Derrida and German philosopher Jürgen Habermas in the summer of 2003 regarding the war in Iraq. They identified six "facets" of European identity: no religion in politics; state correction of the vagaries of the market; the contraction of "the sociopathological consequences of capitalist modernization"[29]; a "preference for the protective guarantees of the welfare state and solidaristic solutions"[30] against "an individualist performance ethos which accepts crass social inequalities"; the abolition of the death penalty; and a "world domestic policy" that renounces the use of force. As Garton Ash concludes, this vision claims that Europe is "*different* from the United States, that in these differences Europe is, on the whole, *better* than the United States, and that a European *identity* can and should be built upon these differences—or superiorities. Europe, in short, is the Not-America."[31]

This EUtopian vision, moreover, is touted not only as superior to America, but also as a model for the whole world to imitate. It is based on a view of the state as a powerful actor in achieving global social justice: "The state," Nicolaides writes, "should fulfill a wide range of socioeconomic and political functions—abroad as well as at home."[32] The social welfare entitlements, for example, that Europeans enjoy should be a goal for all peoples, and act as a limit on the forces of economic globalization whose more ruthless consequences are blamed on American-style capitalism and its ethos of radical individualism.

These entitlements for Europe's citizens are indeed extensive. As T. R. Reid puts it, "In Europe falling into the 'safety net' is more like falling into a large, soft bed with a down comforter for protection against the cold and a matron standing by with a warm cup of tea to soothe discomfort." Universal government-paid health care, of course, is the most famous entitlement. But in other areas of life, Europeans rely on government largess to maintain their lifestyle in the face of adversity. For example, the unemployed don't just get a monthly check to cover living expenses; they get housing, utilities, food, and child care benefits, along with cash payments that on average replace about 80 percent of the employee's income (American benefits cover about half of lost income). Other entitlements include free or extremely inexpensive university education, paid leave for new parents (as high as 80 percent of their salaries), child-care subsidies, benefit checks to parents for each child until age eighteen, expansive sick leave, mandated wage floors, restricted working hours (Europeans work about 400 fewer hours than do Americans), and generous paid vacation and holiday leave (23 days in England, 25 in France, at least 30 in Sweden: Americans average 10).[33]

This is the EUtopia held up as a model for the world: state-subsidized comfort, leisure, security, and social justice at home, and a "postmodern" foreign policy that has transcended force and national self-interest, relying instead on international institutions and diplomacy to keep global order and bestow the EUtopian benefits on the whole world. Schooled by three centuries of slaughter inspired by great-power nationalist ambitions and loyalties, Europeans seemingly have evolved beyond such retrograde passions and institutions into the world dreamed by the Enlightenment, a world without want, injustice, or violence.

Indeed, these enthusiastic descriptions of EUtopia remind one of H. G. Wells's Eloi, the "very beautiful and graceful creatures" whom the Time Traveler from Wells's 1895 novel *The Time Machine* encounters in his visit to the year 802,701 A.D. The delicate, youthful, vegetarian Eloi live in a seeming paradise, a garden world without work or conflict or government: "They spent all their time in playing gently, in bathing in the river, in making love in a half-playful fashion, in eating fruit and sleeping."[34]

At first glance, the Eloi appear to be the culmination of human evolution beyond primitivism and deprivation, a cheering vision of human progress and our destined utopia of pleasure and leisure. But on closer inspection, certain features are troubling. The Eloi are tiny, only four feet tall, soft and hairless, "indescribably frail," like a "beautiful kind of consumptive." They have the intellectual level of a five-year old and are "indolent and easily fatigued." Worse, they are hedonistic narcissists, casually watching one of their fellows drown without interrupting their play. The Time Traveler realizes that rather than the culmination of human evolution, the Eloi represent the devolution of the human race, now "decayed to a mere beautiful futility."[35]

This realization is sharpened to horror when the Time Traveler learns of the Morlocks, "bleached obscene, nocturnal Things" that live underground in ant-like collectives and feed on the effete Eloi like "fatted cattle." The achievement of security and ease had simply rendered the Eloi incapable of defending themselves against their savage predators: "I grieved," the Time Traveler says, "to think how brief the dream of human intellect had been. It had committed suicide. It had set itself steadfastly towards comfort and ease, a balanced society with security and permanency as its watchword, it had attained its hopes—to come to this at last."

Are the denizens of EUtopia the vanguard of human development, showing the world the way to the good life of security, peace, and material abundance and pleasures? Or have they, like the Eloi, chosen the path of slow-motion suicide, trading survival for the good life? And if they are like the Eloi, who or what are the Morlocks waiting to devour their prey?

SNAKES IN THE EUTOPIAN GARDEN

The grand ideals of EUtopia touted by its admirers lose their luster when the actual practice of Europeans states is examined. In foreign policy, for example, we noted above that the E.U. recognizes "supranational constraints on unilateral policies," as Professor Nicolaides put it, and has entered a "postmodern" world where disputes will be adjudicated not by force serving nationalist interests but by transnational institutions employing universal principles enshrined in international law. Yet over the last fifteen years, when the Europeans have gotten their chance to put these ideals into action, their behavior has been something quite different from their rhetoric. During the 1990s, they failed to halt ethnic cleansing and genocide in the Balkans, while in the 2002 run-up to the war in Iraq, naked national self-interest determined the behavior of some European nations rather than allegiance to multilateralism and transnational norms.

When in 1991 the Serbs under Milošević began ethnically cleansing non-Serbs in Bosnia, European leaders believed the time had come to demonstrate that in a "multipolar" post-Cold War world, Europe could resolve a conflict in its own backyard using their non-lethal "postmodern" methods, and so stake a claim to global influence commensurate with America's. In the words of Jacques Chirac in 1995, "The bipolar world we have known is finished, and the world of tomorrow will be multipolar. One of these essential poles will be Europe."[36] The Balkan crisis would be an opportunity to show how "essential" the European pole now was. "If one problem can be solved by the Europeans," Luxembourg's foreign minister Jacques Poos declared, "it is the Yugoslav problem. It is not up to the Americans or anyone else."[37]

The "problem" as it unfolded through the 90s was one of horrific dimensions evocative of Nazi Germany: torture, mutilation, rape, concentration camps with skeletal figures behind barbed wire, locked trains filled with prisoners—the urgency of stopping the horror was visible for years on the international news.[38] And the "postmodern" solutions of the Europeans were completely incapable of stopping the slaughter: "In the case of Bosnia," Robert Lieber writes, "weapons embargoes, Security Council resolutions, the creation of U.N.-protected 'safe areas,' and European intervention under U.N. auspices proved ineffective in halting murderous ethnic violence."[39]

Indeed, these solutions frequently worsened the crisis. The arms embargo merely left the Bosnians more vulnerable, as they were facing what was in effect the old Yugoslav army. The U.N. peacekeepers were virtual hostages, targets to be threatened when necessary, and completely ineffectual at protecting the Bosnians. The U.N. "safe areas" turned out to have Orwellian names, as the concentration of people there merely facilitated their slaughter, as happened in Srebrenica, when ill-armed, out-numbered Dutch "peacekeepers" watched as 7,000 Muslim men were killed. Before it all ended, 200,000 people had died and three million had been displaced. Rather than the "New Europe" of E.U. postmodern pretensions, "This was bad old Europe, as it had not been seen since 1945."[40]

Worse still for those E.U. pretensions, the slaughter in Bosnia and later in Kosovo was stopped with American-led old-fashioned bombing campaigns that concentrated the Serbs' minds wonderfully and brought them to the negotiating table. For the simple fact of the matter, both then and now, is that the Europeans do not have the military capacity to project force in order to stop brutality and slaughter, which means they have no threat of force to give teeth to their non-lethal means of resolving conflict. During the Kosovo crisis, for example, the Europeans had to make "heroic efforts," as the British foreign secretary put it, to deploy a mere 2 percent of their nearly two million troops in uniform as peacekeepers.[41] This meant that the United States' military had to bear the burden of stopping the slaughter. Regarding the 1999 bombing campaign in Kosovo, William Shawcross writes, "The United States flew the overwhelming majority of the missions, and dropped almost all the precision-guided U.S.-made munitions, and most of the targets were generated by U.S. intelligence."[42]

This dependence on an America presumably mired in a retrograde reliance on force that Europe had transcended was a "shocking blow to European honor," as Robert Kagan put it. Europe's most potent military, Great Britain's, could provide a mere 4 percent of both the aircraft and the bombs dropped. Moreover, the U.S. ran the campaign its own way, resisting the numerous European attempts at dilatory half-measures. "For all Europe's great economic power," Kagan concludes of the Balkan crisis, "and for all its success at achieving political union, Europe's military weakness had produced diplomatic weakness and sharply diminished its political influence compared to that of the United States, even in a crisis in Europe."[43]

If the Balkan crisis—a "source of serial humiliation," as Tony

Judt puts it— illustrated the impotence of Europe's postmodern paradigm in the face of determined aggression, the run-up to the Iraq war in late 2002 and early 2003 showed that for all the rhetoric of "supranational restraints on unilateral policies," national self-interest was still the key factor in the foreign policy of many European nations.[44] Only the most gullible Europhile could believe that France's and Germany's opposition to the removal of Saddam Hussein was based on some commitment to transnational "multilateralism" enshrined in international law and validated by the U.N. Security Council imprimatur—which was never sought, by the way, to justify the bombing of Serbia, or the military intervention of the French in their various African ex-colonies. As ever, the needs and interests of individual nations and politicians—particularly the most powerful nations in the E.U., France and Germany—determined the positions those nations took and then camouflaged with the rhetoric of international law and multilateralism.

In Germany, Chancellor Gerhard Schroeder, running for re-election in the summer of 2002, needed an issue to deflect attention from his party's dismal record on reenergizing the German economy and putting to work some of the four million unemployed. By campaigning against the coming war in Iraq, despite assurances to President Bush in May that he wouldn't, Schroeder tapped into the anti-Americanism in German society partly created by resentment against Germany's huge debt of obligation to the United States. "Some Germans," a German editor is quoted as saying, "have never forgotten being humiliated by gum-chewing black Americans who 'liberated' them from Hitler."[45] Not content with registering disapproval of American plans to eliminate Hussein, Germany actively campaigned against a Security Council resolution approving the use of force in Iraq. The German ambassador to the U.N. pressured non-permanent Security Council members like Mexico, Chile, Cameroon, and Angola; and Germany joined France and Belgium in formally objecting to a proposal for NATO to send defensive equipment to Turkey, which wanted assurances that it would be supported by its fellow NATO members if attacked for supporting the war against Hussein.[46] This obstructionism had nothing to do with some new "postmodern" foreign policy paradigm, and everything to do with political necessity and national *amour propre*.[47]

In France, too, the old-fashioned electoral needs of a politician were a factor in the nation's foreign policy position. But there were other equally old-fashioned interests involved—money and national influence. As a veto-bearing member of the U.N. Security Council, France was in a greater position than Germany to protect those interests even if it meant failing to disarm a proven mass-murderer who had violated sixteen U.N. Security Council resolutions—so much for respecting international law and institutions.

The great apostle of international law and multilateralism, French President Jacques Chirac, was in fact one of Saddam Hussein's best international friends for three decades: Chirac once called the butcher of Baghdad "a personal friend and a great statesman" who enjoyed the Frenchman's "esteem, consideration, and affection."[48] In 1974, then Prime Minister Chirac traveled to Iraq where he negotiated with then Vice President Saddam Hussein to sell nuclear reactors to Iraq. In 1975, France agreed to sell two reactors to oil-rich Iraq, one with enough weapons-grade uranium for three or four nuclear devices. Hussein stated publicly that the agreement was the "very first concrete step toward production of the Arab atomic bomb."[49] The Israelis destroyed this reactor in 1981, doing the civilized world a huge favor. But Chirac gained personal political advantages from his relationship with Hussein and his status as head of the "unofficial 'Iraq lobby' in France." After his forced resignation as prime minister in 1976, Chirac stayed afloat politically with money rumored to have come from Hussein.[50]

But the nuclear reactor was just one small part of France's weapons trade with Hussein. In the same deal that sold the nuclear reactor to Iraq, France sold another $1.5 billion worth of weapons, including the Mirage F1, France's most advanced jet fighter at the time, along with an air-defense system, surface-to-air missiles, and advanced electronics. This was just the beginning of French arms sales to Iraq, which reached $20 billion worth of the most sophisticated weaponry, including "thousands of HOT and Milan anti-tank missiles, Roland 2 air defense systems, and Gazelle helicopters." As Kenneth Timmerman notes, "Iraq was in effect subsidizing the French Defense Ministry."

By 1983, Iraq was buying more than half of all French arms exports.[51] In return, the French received oil and lucrative contracts to develop Iraqi oil fields. And of course, in the decade between Gulf Wars I and II, France continued to do business with Hussein's regime, over a billion dollars worth in 2002, not counting the nearly four billion dollars reaped through the corrupt U.N. oil-for-food program, in which eleven Frenchmen participated, including a former Minister of the Interior and two *ambassadeurs de France*.[52] But the lucrative contracts to develop oil fields perhaps influenced France's behavior the most, as well as the vision of renewed arms sales once sanctions on Iraq were lifted. In 1994, oil giants Total SA and Elf had negotiated contracts to develop the Nahr Umar and Manjoon fields; the Total SA deal was worth $50 billion over seven years—with oil at $20 a barrel. Needless to say, these deals would be worthless if Hussein was removed from power.[53]

It is no surprise, then, that before the U.S. invasion France was actively working to lift the U.N. sanctions on Iraq and to weaken the U.N. weapons inspections, and then furiously opposed America's decision to remove a homicidal autocrat. Deep-seated anti-

Americanism—after war broke out, a quarter of the French wanted Hussein to win, and foreign minister Dominique de Villepin said that an American victory was "not desirable"—and fear of France's restless Muslim population also contributed to France's decision to oppose America.[54] Rather than an Enlightenment commitment to "post-national" multilateralism based on international law and institutions, France and Chirac were pursuing their own political and economic interests: "The long friendship with Saddam, commercial considerations, the response to the *le défi Américain*, and concern over the reactions of France's Muslims—all these played a part in Chirac's calculations in summer 2002."[55]

The behavior of France and Germany will surprise no one who understands that nations pursue their interests by whatever means available, depending on how strong or weak they are vis-à-vis their rivals. The E.U. recourse to multilateralism and transnational institutions is as much the reflection of European weakness as of idealism: "Europe's relative weakness," Kagan notes, "has understandably produced a powerful European interest in building a world where military strength and hard power matter less than economic and soft power."[56] Given that the E.U. nations' military spending combined is a bit more than half that of the United States, it is indeed understandable that such "military pygmies," as NATO Secretary-General Lord Robertson once put it, pursue their national, political, and economic interests through other means, and use these means to hinder and impede the United States when its pursuit of *its* interests conflict with those of Europe.[57]

At any rate, the actual behavior of Europe certainly does not support any notion of a new, enlightened paradigm for creating global order and resolving conflict that eschews force and relies instead on diplomacy and transnational institutions. That aspect of the European Dream is an illusion. The truth is closer to that expressed by George Washington during the Revolutionary War, regarding the young nation's new alliance with France: "It is a maxim founded on the universal experience of mankind, that no nation can be trusted farther than it is bounded by its interests."[58]

The rosy portrait of EUtopia's domestic bliss offered by admirers like Jeremy Rifkin is equally illusory. It certainly is hard to square with the dismal estimation of modern Europe found in some of the continent's most important writers. Two novelists in particular, one from Germany and one from France, offer a more pessimistic vision of the "postmodern" E.U. paradise, one in many ways evocative of Wells's prophecy of European decline.

In the novels of German writer W. G. Sebald, a once magnificent European civilization has fractured into a heap of broken fragments that lack all coherence and meaning and so are slipping into oblivion. His rootless protagonists wander through this shattered cultural landscape and attempt to restore through memory that lost meaning, only to find at the end of their search the dark master-narrative of modern Europe: the war and genocide that filled Europe with corpses and refugees and displaced persons. The survivors of that cataclysm are no longer at home in a world in which their identities have been deformed or lost, leaving them, like the character Austerlitz from the novel of the same name, prey to "some soul-destroying and inexorable force," a "dreadful torpor that heralds the disintegration of the personality." Their lives now are trapped in "a constant process of obliteration" that leaves them incapable even of staying alive: if someone came to "lead me away to a place of execution," Austerlitz says, "I would have gone meekly, without a word, without so much as opening my eyes."[59]

Sebald's novels abound in architectural metaphors, often accompanied by grainy, black-and-white photographs, that capture the dilapidated state of European civilization in which such lost souls like Austerlitz wander. In *Austerlitz*, a once-grand English country house now seems "as if silent horror had seized upon [it] at the prospect of its imminent and shameful end," the bits and pieces of European high culture that it contains now broken and covered with sheep dung. Such buildings, constructed by a European civilization confident in its power and superiority, now serve only as decaying reminders of that lost glory, like the neo-baroque Central Station in Antwerp, in which the waiting passengers seemed "somehow miniaturized" by the lofty dome 200 feet above them. Like Wells's Eloi, they are "the last members of a diminutive race which had perished or had been expelled from its homeland."[60]

Sebald's lyrical melancholy for the broken grandeur of Europe is nowhere to be found in the work of French novelist Michel Houellebecq. There the fragmentation of European civilization leaves people no meaning in life, no way of connecting with other people except through their physical appetites and pleasures, especially sex, no matter how impersonal, humiliating, or sordid. In *Platform*, Houellebecq's grand metaphor is not the lost architectural grandeur or lovely fragments of European civilization that Sebald mourns and memorializes, but the sex-tourism industry, where Europe's spiritual emptiness and hedonism intersect with the forces of economic globalization.

Houellebecq's narrator Michel embodies many of the pathologies of postmodern EUtopian man. Reduced to mere appetite and pleasure, and cut off from meaningful community or connection with something greater than himself, the narcissistic Michel, indifferent to others, relies solely on the "meager compensation" of sexual pleasure to compensate for humans having been created "short-lived, vain, and cruel."[61] The France in which he lives is "utterly sinister and bureaucratic," a place where under "placid socialism" materialism is the highest good and "Pleasure is a right," as the advertising slogan of a sex-tourism company puts it.[62] Yet at the same time, Paris is terrorized by immigrant gangs and reports of "professors being stabbed, schoolteacher being raped, fire engines attacked with Molotov cocktails, handicapped people thrown through train windows because they had 'looked the wrong way' at some gang leader," a description prophetic of the November, 2005 immigrant riots in Paris.[63]

Michel sees clearly that his own and his contemporaries' amoral, useless existence is the consequence of the bounty created by his European forbears, who "believed in the superiority of their civilization" and had "invented dreams, progress, utopia, the future." But their "civilizing mission," their "innocent sense of their natural right to dominate the world and direct the path of history had disappeared." What remains are the freedom, leisure, and wealth they created, the capital being squandered by their descendents, who like Michel have lost "those qualities of intelligence and determination." All that is left are material pleasures: "As a decadent European, conscious of my approaching death, and given over entirely to selfishness, I could see no reason to deprive myself of such things." But Michel knows that living for pleasure is a cultural dead end: "I was aware, however, that such a situation was barely tenable, that people like me were incapable of ensuring the survival of a society. Perhaps, more simply, we were unworthy of life."[64]

Yet physical pleasure cannot give life meaning even for a selfish hedonist, as Michel learns when the woman with whom he thought he had forged a meaningful bond based on their mutual obsession with sex is murdered in Thailand by Islamic terrorists, those true believers who still possess the transcendent meaning and purpose in life that Europeans have lost. After his recovery from the attack, Michel stays on in Thailand to commit slow-motion suicide. Before dying, he leaves a chilling epitaph for the West: "To the end, I will remain a child of Europe, of worry and shame. I have no message of hope to deliver. For the West, I do not feel hatred. At most I feel a great contempt. I know only that every single one of us reeks of selfishness, masochism, and death.

We have created a system in which it has simply become impossible to live."[65] Like Wells's Eloi, postmodern Europeans have sacrificed the values and beliefs that ensure survival for comfort and pleasure, a trade-off that can end only in extinction.

Novelists, of course, speak for themselves, yet the rootlessness, despair, and failure of community Sebald and Houellebecq chronicle are reinforced by other evidence less subjective and impressionistic. A recent poll cited by columnist Mark Steyn reports that in France, 29 percent of those polled felt optimistic about the future, while in Germany only 15 percent did so. Meanwhile in violence-ridden Iraq, 69 percent were optimistic that things will approve.[66] Likewise a 2003 Harris poll found that while 57 percent of Americans are satisfied with their lives, only 14 percent of the French, 17 percent of the Germans, and 16 percent of the Italians are.[67] Suicide rates are equally revealing: in many European countries, suicide is the second leading cause of death, after accidents, and France's suicide rate is about twice that of the United States', as are Belgium's, Luxembourg's, Finland's, Austria's, and Switzerland's.[68] Rates of emigration from Europe to America, even as hardly any Americans immigrate to Europe, also suggest that the "European Dream" is not so attractive to many of those who live it. Before 9/11, European immigration to the U.S. rose by 16 percent; of the two million Germans who have left their country, most come to the U.S. Even given the visa restrictions after the terrorist attacks, rates are starting to climb again. Many of these immigrants are coming from the old Soviet Union and Eastern Europe, bypassing the closer E.U. paradise for the culture presumably mired in outmoded paradigms.[69]

The E.U. managers themselves acknowledge this pervasive malaise afflicting their citizens. A survey conducted in 2006 by Eurobarometer, the E.U.'s own polling service, reports that the tone of respondents is "mostly one of anxiety. In all or almost all countries—albeit with varying intensity—fears and uncertainties largely predominate and are moreover articulated with greater precision and conviction than is the case for hopes, which are expressed in a much more hesitant and vague manner: this anxiety is focused on concrete perspectives, anchored in the objective reality of the present, whilst hopes are in the form of desires or personal wishes, and reflect the psychology of each respondent, as well as the tendency of their 'temperament' towards confidence and optimism. In this case, a large number acknowledge that they are 'pessimistic' for themselves and/or, more seriously, for their children."[70] As *New York Times* reporter Richard Bernstein has noted, "there seems to be no energy and no political will directed toward what used to be enthusiastically called the European project."[71]

This book will explore in more detail the various problems that diminish the luster of the European Dream and challenge its status as a model for the United States. Rampant secularization in Europe has led to spiritual impoverishment and a materialist culture of pleasure, leaving Europeans unsure about what is worth fighting, killing, and dying for, not to mention rendering them incapable of defending their own civilization against those who want to destroy it. Old socialist-inspired assumptions continue to drive government interference in the economy and social life, with chronic unemployment, punitive rates of taxation, and expensive social welfare entitlements, with the result that many E.U. economies, particularly the powerhouses France, Germany, and England, are increasingly incapable of competing in a rapidly globalizing and interconnected economy. A dwindling population exacerbates these problems, as Europeans are not reproducing at replacement rates, raising the question of where the workers will come from to provide the revenues for generous retirement and other benefits. Meanwhile, a growing cohort of fecund, unassimilated, underemployed Muslim immigrants continues to fester, its marginalization worsened by self-loathing Third-Worldism and boutique multiculturalism on the part of Europeans who cannot praise the superiority of their own culture. Marginalized Muslim immigrants, moreover, account for much of the crime in Europe and a resurgent anti-Semitism. A neo-fascist resurgence of nationalist xenophobia may be one response to the increasing impact of disaffected Muslims on European life. Finally, an irrational anti-Americanism, the product of resentment and envy, prohibit many Europeans from seeing the United States as a model for how to integrate immigrants and unleash the entrepreneurial energy of individuals and free markets.

The European Dream, then, may be the dream of Wells's Eloi, an illusion of enlightened prosperity and peace masking the darker forces slowly destroying it from within.

The Death of God and Some Failing Gods

EUROPE ON THE BRINK

THE PLACE OF Europe in the world today, though obviously still significant, is very different from its overwhelming global dominance in 1914 on the brink of the First World War. At that time, Europe—one-quarter of the world's population, compared to 7 percent today—indeed bestrode the globe as a colossus. Through its colonial empires, European nations controlled, to some degree, three-fourths of the world's cultures and peoples. England alone was in possession of a quarter, while its navy ruled the oceans.

In one respect, however, E.U. Europe today resembles the Europe of 1914: its optimism for the future based on a transnational interconnection of states whose interests are best served by peaceful cooperation rather than militaristic nationalism. In 1914, this optimism was underwritten by "peaceful productivity so dependent on international exchange and co-operation that a belief in the impossibility of general war seemed the most conventional of wisdoms," a belief articulated in Norman Angell's 1910 best-seller *The Great Illusion*.[1] International organizations and agreements sprang up to formalize the interdependence of nations, transnational treaties were written to eradicate slavery and international prostitution, and an International Court was created to limit the use of the new military technologies and to promote peaceful solutions to conflict. The free movement of resources, goods, capital, ideas, and people throughout the world —"globalization" was in many ways more advanced then than it is now—also promoted the notion of war's obsolescence, as did political and philosophical ideas that made material comfort, rational calculation of self-interest, and scientific rationalism the prime engines of human behavior.[2] The Enlightenment liberation of mankind from religious superstition and retrograde traditions had seemingly led to a world of technological advance and material improvement. And this progress could only accelerate, eventually bringing the fruits of advanced civilization, social improvement, and material prosperity to the whole world.

Yet lurking beneath this façade of progressive improvement, forces long at work within European culture would explode in the balmy summer of 1914. The First World War, of course, was devastating beyond anything Europe had ever experienced. By the time it was all over, twenty million soldiers and civilians had died, another twenty-one million had been wounded, and the post-war Spanish flu pandemic took another twenty million lives.[3] Moreover, the dead were concentrated in a particular cohort: one in three young males was lost to the war: "Little wonder," historian John Keegan writes, "the post-war world spoke of a 'lost generation,' that its parents were united by shared grief and the survivors proceeded into the life that followed with a sense of inexplicable escape, often tinged by guilt, sometimes by rage and desire for revenge."[4]

In addition to the butcher's bill, the Great War destroyed four empires, created a raft of new, mostly unstable nations, and unleashed nationalist, ethnic, religious, and ideological forces with which we are still dealing today. The Second World War, which killed fifty million and reached levels of destruction and genocidal murder unprecedented in human history, was a continuation of the First, and it makes perfect sense to speak of both wars as one, the twentieth century's Thirty Years War. The Great War was also the midwife of Nazism and Bolshevist communism, and the concentration camps, corpses, displaced persons, and broken lives both species of totalitarianism left behind. The ill-conceived and hasty abandonment of European colonies, particularly in Africa, left those peoples with the worst of both worlds, their own culture's dysfunctions rendered even more toxic by badly digested European ideologies, particularly nationalism and socialism. The fifty-year Cold War followed, with its numerous proxy wars, revolutions, postcolonial chaos, and the chronic threat of nuclear annihilation. And the dissolution of the Ottoman Empire left us with the modern Middle East, the current font of global disorder. German historian Fritz Stern aptly has called the Great War "the first calamity of the twentieth century ... from which all other calamities sprang."[5]

Why did these catastrophes happen? "Why," Catholic theologian George Weigel asks, "did a century that began with confident predictions about a maturing humanity reaching new heights of civilizational accomplishment produce in Europe, within four decades, two world wars, three totalitarian systems, a Cold War threatening global catastrophe, oceans of blood, mountains of corpses, Auschwitz and the Gulag?"[6]

The causes of the Great War are many, but surely the increasing secularization of Europe and the decline of traditional religious authority throughout the nineteenth century were in part responsible for the willingness of Europeans both to go to war and to continue fighting even when the conflict settled into a horrific stalemate marked by seemingly pointless slaughter. "World War I," Weigel writes, "was the product of a crisis of civilizational morality, a failure of moral reason in a culture that had given the world the very concept of moral reason." That "crisis of civilizational morality" that followed the banishment of God from public culture, Weigel adds, has led to a similar crisis today: "It was only after 1991 [the end of the Cold War], when the seventy-seven-year political-military crisis that began in 1914 had ended, that the long-term effects of Europe's 'rage of self-mutilation' [as Aleksandr Solzhenitsyn put it] could come to the surface of history and be seen for what they were—and what they are."[7]

Indeed, today God has been banished from European public life. In addition to the low level of church attendance mentioned earlier (in Western Europe, around 5 percent), opinion polls reveal the underlying attitudes that explain the empty churches and cathedrals across the continent. Percentages of people who tell pollsters that religion is very important in their lives range from 9 percent in Denmark to a third in Catholic Italy and Poland; in the U.S. 60 percent say religion is very important. And while 50 percent of Americans go to church every week, in the Netherlands, Great Britain, Germany, Sweden, and Denmark, fewer than 10 percent attend once a month.[8] Unsurprisingly, fewer Europeans believe in sin: only 57 percent of Spaniards, 55 percent of Germans, 40 percent of the French, and 30 percent of Swedes.[9] T. R. Reid writes about attending Sunday services in churches all over Europe and being struck by "how beautiful those structures were, and how empty." Stockholm's St. Jacob's Church, with a capacity of nine hundred, had twenty-nine people when Reid visited, and in England's famed Canterbury Cathedral during one morning-prayer service, he counted thirteen, the number swelling at midday only because of an influx of tourists.[10] Europeans may not have become outright atheists, as Tony Blankley argues from his own analysis of the European Values Study.[11] But the surviving faithful tend to be concentrated among the aged, the rural, and some Eastern European countries.[12] These low levels of church attendance and the relentless "de-Christianization" of the European public square, starkly evident in the grand cathedrals filled these days mostly with tourists, suggest that whatever spiritual beliefs Europeans profess to pollsters are worn very lightly.

Private belief aside, the "Christophobic" nature of European public life, to use legal historian J. H. H. Weiler's term, is apparent everywhere, surfacing in issues both trivial and important. In the Netherlands, Dutch orthographers ordered that starting in October 2006, "Christ" would be written with a lower-case "c," and "Jews" with a lower-case "j" when referring to the religion. When Slovakia signed a concordat with the Vatican that the government would respect the choice of doctors not to perform abortions because of moral convictions, the E.U. thundered that abortion is an "international human right" doctors have no choice but to recognize, whatever their religious convictions.[13] In England, clerics in the Anglican Church dismiss the Crucifixion and Resurrection as metaphors, "cathedrals have been converted into nightclubs, the crucifix is a fashion accessory, and the word *Religion* is a brand name for young women's dancewear."[14]

Worse still, the church has often taken the lead in secularizing itself by shifting its mission from saving souls and ministering to the flock, to changing the world and agitating for "social justice." Particularly in England, the nostrums of liberal and leftist ideology have become the new doctrines, with all the self-loathing guilt that accompanies the West's loss of faith in its own institutions. Speaking in Cairo in 2005, the Archbishop of Canterbury apologized to the world because "the Church had taken 'cultural captives' by exporting hymns and liturgies to remote parts of the world."[15] In some instances this guilty doubt has metamorphosed into cheerful disbelief: the Anglican primate of Scotland, presiding at a funeral for British foreign secretary Robin Cook, described himself as "an agnostic Anglican, taking the service in a Presbyterian church, for a dead atheist politician. And I thought that was just marvelous."[16]

Elsewhere in Europe, crude caricatures of Christian doctrine and symbols are casually accepted. Such blasphemy, Weigel notes, is "tolerated in European popular culture in a way that similar defamation of Judaism and Islam would never be."[17] The refusal to acknowledge the Christian roots of Europe in the E.U. Constitution mentioned earlier showed the same disdain for Christianity among the Eurocratic elite, some of whom called the demand to acknowledge Europe's Christian roots "absurd," a "huge mistake," and a "joke."[18] This hostility to Christianity's presence in the European public square was also revealed in late 2004, when Italian Catholic philosopher Rocco Buttiglione's nomination to be the commissioner of justice in the European Commission was attacked and derailed because his Christian convictions about homosexuality and the nature of marriage were deemed "in direct contradiction of European law."[19]

Rather than an expression of tolerance for nonbelievers and non-Christians, the E.U.'s refusal to acknowledge the historical fact of Europe's cultural debt to Christianity is, according to Pope Benedict XVI, "the expression of a consciousness that would like to see God eradicated once and for all from the public life of humanity and shut up in the subjective sphere of cultural residues from the past."[20] Claire Berlinski's description of a de-Christianized England rings true for Western Europe as a whole: "British Christianity has become a vaporous shadow of its former self."[21]

The powerful opening sequence of *La Dolce Vita*, Federico Fellini's cinematic portrait of postwar Italian decadence and moral exhaustion, shows a statue of Christ dangling from a helicopter carrying it away from Rome. How was it that Europeans allowed God to disappear from their lives?

* * *

The Death of God

Murdering God

When Nietzsche in 1887 made his famous declaration that "God is dead"—that, as he elaborated later, "the belief in the Christian god has become unbelievable," for "God is no more than a faded word today, not even a concept"—he was merely stating the obvious conclusion of a process that had been unfolding for more than a century.[22] Nietzsche's further comments make it clear, moreover, that God's death wasn't from "natural causes," the end result of mankind's increasing enlightenment, but was an act of premeditated murder: "Wither is God?" the "madman" in a parable asks. "I will tell you. We have killed him—you and I. All of us are his murderers. . . . God is dead. God remains dead. And we have killed him."[23]

An act of murder is Nietzsche's accurate description of the culmination of the long process of secularization, or "the growing tendency of mankind to do without religion," as Owen Chadwick defines it, that Europe had been fitfully going through since the eighteenth-century Enlightenment.[24] It was then that thinkers began to conceive of a political and social life devoid of God and the church and all the fossilized traditional wisdom and prejudices now dismissed as irrational impediments to mankind's progress and happiness. In their place, human reason and experience were now exalted as the royal road to the truth about humanity and the world. For contrary to Christianity's belief in man's sinful nature and the limits of human knowing, the Enlightenment assumed that most humans are essentially good and able to acquire useful truths about themselves and the world, truths that would lead to greater progress and freedom.

From the Enlightenment came the dream of human perfection achieved not through the irrational, incoherent mysteries of Christianity promising salvation in some fictive paradise, but through the activity of rational men using their knowledge to manipulate both the natural and social worlds and thus create happiness in the here and now. Isaiah Berlin summarizes this Enlightenment optimism, which has come to dominate the modern world:

> The behaviour of human beings, both individually and in the aggregate, is in principle intelligible, if the facts are observed patiently and intelligently, hypotheses formulated and verified, laws established, with the same degree of genius and success—and why not?—as had attended the great discoveries of physics, astronomy, and chemistry; and seemed likely soon to bring about similar triumphs in the realm of biology, physiology, and psychology. The success of physics seemed to give reason for optimism: once appropriate social laws were discovered, rational organization would take the place of blind improvisation, and men's wishes, within the limits of the uniformities of nature, could in principle all be made to come true.[25]

To the "enlightened," the greatest enemy of this program was the church and its minions. It was in the church's interests to keep people cowering in superstitious fear and material deprivation, enslaved to doctrines that justified tyranny and oppression. Thus, the Enlightenment philosophers and those following them "formed something like a regular plan for the destruction of the Christian religion," English political philosopher Edmund Burke wrote.[26] As the nineteenth century advanced, people of faith increasingly were viewed by "progressive" thinkers as "shamans or witch doctors from savage tribes whom one humors until one can dress them in trousers and send them to school," as Polish poet Czeslaw Milosz put it.[27]

Killing off the Christian God, however, did not destroy religion. The need to believe in a truth that validates one's values and that organizes one's life and gives it—and its inevitable end—meaning is too ingrained in human nature to be swept away by removing the traditional expressions of that need, even for intellectuals who fancy themselves cool rationalists. The discrediting of Christianity's public authority merely created a vacuum which over the last two centuries has been filled by numerous pseudo-religions, with results more disastrous and bloody than all the alleged crimes of Christianity. For, as G. K. Chesterton pointed out, "When men stop believing in God they don't believe in nothing; they believe in anything."

THE FAILED IDOLS OF SCIENTISM

The French Revolution was in part the child of the Enlightenment, and the first concrete expression of its hostility to religion: "The philosophes," historian Peter Gay writes, "chased the sacred from its privileged sanctuary and treated it as a fact—as a symptom of hysteria, a device of political management, a mark of illiteracy, or a stage in historical development."[28] Thus, it is no surprise that the overthrow of the *ancien régime* included a virulent assault on the beliefs, institutions, and authority of the church and Christianity, once the philosophers had prepared the way intellectually. Church properties were seized and auctioned off, religious orders abolished, religious and priests massacred, nuns and priests tied together naked and thrown into water to drown (the "republican marriage"), and churches desecrated and despoiled to the accompaniment of sordid blasphemy. Meanwhile, the eradication of traditional Christianity from public life proceeded apace, most notoriously in the rejection of dating anno Domini, "in the year of the Lord," time now beginning anew with Year 1 of the Revolution.

The Revolution did not just attempt to cleanse French society of the church, but also tried to turn the revolution and the state it created into a new religion, illustrating Owen Chadwick's observation that "secularization is a religious process, instead of an irreligious."[29] The revolutionary faith was utopian in its novel aim to create absolute equality among men, and redemptive in that it thought men could be "born again" and thus shed the sins of its corrupt nature under the *ancien régime*. To create a public expression of this new faith, the revolutionaries plundered Greco-Roman paganism and Christianity alike to cobble together a pseudo-religion that worshipped the revolution and its various abstractions and virtues by means of public festivals and spectacles celebrated in cathedrals like Notre Dame, renamed the Temple of Reason.

At first, this new faith was melded with traditional Catholicism, but that synthesis failed. "So why not," Michael Burleigh writes, "elevate the Revolution itself into the religion? After all, it had its creeds, liturgies and sacred texts, its own vocabulary of virtues and vices, and, last but not least, the ambition of regenerating mankind itself."[30] And this Manichean creed had its "holy wars" as well: against the revolution's "heretics," guillotined en masse; against the "apostates" in the Vendée, two hundred fifty thousand of whom were massacred for revolting against the new faith; and against the "infidel" monarchies of Europe, in a series of wars that left millions dead from Spain to Russia. One lasting effect of this religion of revolution was the legitimizing of revolutionary violence as a redemptive and regenerating force, as long as it is in the service of the leftist view of historical progress. Revolution became a substitute for God, or as François Furet puts it, "an additional negation of divinity, which had for so long been the sole master of the human theater," and thus a way of "reinvesting religious ambitions in politics, since revolution itself is a quest for grace."[31]

The attempt to elevate the revolution into a faith illustrates the fundamental basis of all pseudo-religions: they make man himself into an object of worship, attributing to humans all the powers once possessed by God. Nietzsche drew this obvious conclusion from God's death, calling on the "Higher Men" to take His place: "Only since he has lain in the grave have you again been resurrected. Only now does the great noontide come, only now does the Higher Man become—lord and master!"[32] Yet Nietzsche was merely stating more theatrically what many nineteenth-century intellectuals before him were in effect doing: making a god of humanity so that people supposedly could regain their freedom and achieve the greatness they were due, once the obstacles of God and church had been removed.

The core belief of most of these new religions was a fervent faith in the efficacy of human reason and scientific knowledge. Yet the originators of such creeds still acknowledged the social utility of traditional religion, understandable given how widespread religious belief remained among the masses. What was needed was a new faith, one that could substitute for an outmoded, oppressive traditional Christianity and that would answer to what was believed to be man's potential for progress and happiness. For, as Isaiah Berlin describes the thinking of the early nineteenth-century philosopher Henri de Saint-Simon, "one cannot live by technological wisdom alone; . . . something must be done to stimulate the feelings, the emotions, the religious instincts of mankind." Saint-Simon is the first inventor of a rationalist pseudo-religion, a "substitute for religion, that secularized, humanized, de-theologicalized variant of Christianity of which so many versions began to circulate in the nineteenth century and after."[33]

The positivism of Saint-Simon's admirer Auguste Comte was such a creed: "The essence of his Religion of Humanity," as Burleigh describes it, "was to redirect mankind's spiritual energies away from the transcendental and towards the creation of a happier and more moral life here on earth through the worship of the best in man himself."[34] Given that, as Comte put it, "God has gone, unquestionably and forever," positivism was set to take its place, an alternative creed complete with festivals, saints, "social sacraments," a "priesthood of humanity" (scientists), and even an afterlife of sorts. Like most pseudo-religions, the fundamental aim was to take over the social and political power once wielded by the church: "Today the servants of Humanity," Comte asserted prophetically, "are ousting the servants of God, root and branch, from all control of public affairs." Never lacking in confidence, Comte further predicted, in this case erroneously, "I am convinced that before the year 1860 I shall be preaching positivism at Notre Dame as the only real and complete religion."[35] The positivism of Comte may have failed to become the universal faith of his dreams, yet his vision of a Europe in which the "servants of God" have been banished "root and branch" from the public square, their place taken by technocrats and managers, has become a reality.

In contrast to those like Comte who wanted to create some sort of "religion of humanity" to replace Christianity, many nineteenth-century rationalists made science itself a sort of faith, thus elevating scientism into a pseudo-religion. Some were quite frank about the displacement of faith by science: Darwin's cousin Francis Galton believed scientists should become a "new priesthood," and German pathologist Rudolf Vischow said "science has become a religion for us."[36] They were radical materialists, inspired by Charles Darwin to believe that humans were mere animals, their minds and choices nothing more than the byproduct of physiological processes and the laws of nature, as Darwin's German popularizer Karl Vogt indicated when he famously said, "Thoughts come out of the brain as gall from the liver, or urine from the kidneys."[37] This knowledge based on materialism, moreover, promised an emancipation and progress long retarded by the superstitions of traditional Christianity. Anticipating Nietzsche's "Higher Men," another German doctor and popularizer of Darwin, Ludwig Büchner, proclaimed, "Not as the humble and submissive slave of a supernatural master, nor as the helpless toy in the hands of heavenly powers, but as a proud and free son of Nature, understanding her laws and knowing how to tutor them to his own use, does the creature of modern civilization, the Freethinker, appear."[38]

These nineteenth-century "evangelical atheists" have their counterparts today among those who reduce all reality to matter and then claim to know the truth of human nature and behavior.[39] And this truth supposedly has practical applications through techniques and technologies that can deliver progress and happiness in this world, if only the elite "technicians of the soul" are given the power once reserved for priests. In other words, materialist atheism is a pseudo-religion, as it must be, since to claim all reality is material, or that God or the soul does not exist, is to make a metaphysical rather than a scientific claim.

An even more pernicious leftover of all these nineteenth-century attempts to remove God and Christianity from social and political life is the faith in centralized planning and the rational organization of human society and psychology, the idolization of technique, and the acceptance of power in the hands of a quasi-priestly elite that will all create heaven on earth, the utopia of peace, equality, and justice—once those resisting the creation of this terrestrial paradise are gotten out of the way. The "religion of humanity" thus ends more autocratic and tyrannous—and bloodthirsty — than any traditional faith ever dreamed of being.

The persistence of this mentality can be seen everywhere today in the West, but particularly in Europe: a social and political order creating universal happiness, peace, and prosperity—these days institutionalized in the E.U.— is obtainable through knowledge

and rational technique alone, provided that the retrogressive superstitions of Christianity and their baneful effects are driven from
the public square, and power is put into the hands of an enlightened elite who can lead the masses to the promised land.

POLITICAL RELIGIONS: FASCISM

The malign consequences of positivism and scientism, however,
can not compare to the disasters wrought by "political religions,"
those revolutions, ideologies, and movements that borrow the
trappings of faith to attract and energize followers and pursue
grandiose ambitions of universal regeneration and the creation of
paradise on earth, all predicated on mythic assumptions about
human nature and possibility.[40] Since these beliefs about human
nature and the human condition cannot be proven by science,
their adherents act on faith in the truth of these beliefs. As we
have seen, the French Revolution is the first of this sort of pseudo-
religion, "a new kind of religion," Tocqueville described it, "an
incomplete religion, it is true, without God, without ritual, and
without life after death, but one which nevertheless, like Islam,
flooded the earth with its soldiers, apostles, and martyrs."[41]

Many people have described the two great twentieth-century
totalitarian political movements, fascism and communism, as
political religions that flourished in the civilizational breakdown
following the Great War. As the German journalist Frederick
Voigt wrote in 1938, "Both [Marxism and Nazism] are messianic
and socialistic. Both reject the Christian knowledge that all are
under sin and both see in good and evil principles of class or race.
Both are despotic in their methods and their mentality. Both have
enthroned the modern Caesar, collective man, the implacable
enemy of the individual soul. Both would render unto this Caesar the things which are God's. Both would make man master of

his own destiny, establish the Kingdom of Heaven in this world. Neither will hear of any Kingdom that is not of this world."[42]

As collectivist ideologies, both communism and fascism hated the bourgeoisie, the epitome of commerce and individualism: fascists because the bourgeoisie are bound by money and contracts rather than by the communal bonds of the folk; communists because they are merely a doomed phase of history to be displaced by the proletariat. Both despised liberal democracy with its notions of civil liberties and private property, and both "set in motion the destruction of the civil order by the absolute submission of individuals to the ideology and the terror of the party-state."[43] Both were revolutionary, and so tapped into the "revolutionary passion," as Furet calls it, "the central and ultimately the universal figure on the European stage."[44] And most important, both viewed human beings as "expendable raw material for the construction of a new social order and the creation of a 'new man,'" and so both were totalitarian regimes with unlimited authority that employed terror, torture, murder, and the "big lie" as the instruments of a "religion of power" dedicated to the fulfillment of history.[45] And both were born in Europe, and in Europe reached their bloody culmination.

At the heart of fascism is what historian Robert Paxton calls "passionate nationalism."[46] Rather than Christianity's universal community of the saved, the unique, distinct "people" and "race" now become the locus of individual salvation and regeneration, the larger whole into which each person should submerge himself, and there find his authentic identity and meaning and be reborn as a purified "new man." This process was abetted by emotionally charged and theatrical public rites, rituals, and spectacles. These "chosen people," however, are threatened by the alien "damned" whose racial or ideological degeneracy compromises the purity of the people, left vulnerable in a fallen modern world of economic disorder, social disintegration, rapid change, moral confusion, and rootless individualism. The revealed truth of this nationalist salvation comes from a messianic leader and prophet who embodies the people's aspirations and identity. If the people submit without question to the messiah's leadership, he can lead them to the earthly promised land of racial regeneration and primacy. And the group's superiority as the chosen saved justifies their domination of others through sacralized violence.

Nazi Germany, of course, was the most destructive and murderous realization of these fascistic elements. One has only to watch Leni Riefenstahl's *Triumph of the Will*, her cinematic record of the 1934 Nazi party rally in Nuremberg, to see how Nazism caricatured the trappings of religion to bind its adherents to Hitler's will: the Führer's descent from the clouds, like a god coming to earth; the procession through the old cathedral city's streets lined with adoring postulants; Albert Speer's "cathedrals of light" accompanied by the world's largest electric organ; the celebration of and homage paid to the party's "saints" and "martyrs"; the ritualistic Nazi salutes and torchlight parades—all evoke a pseudo-faith in which the individual is absorbed into the collective whole just as the Christian becomes one with the church, the body of Christ. "The fundamental structure of the Nazi creed," Michael Burleigh writes, "was soteriological, a redemptive story of suffering and deliverance, a sentimental journey from misery to glory, from division to mystic unity based on the blood bond that linked souls."[47] Yet Nazism was a faith predicated on hatred and death, not love and eternal life, and the toll of its "holy war" vastly outstrips the deaths caused by Christians who over the centuries distorted their faith to kill in the pursuit of more worldly aims.

In Europe the horrors of Nazism have so discredited any political program based on biological racism that a fascist resurgence of that sort is extremely unlikely. Neo-Nazi and neo-Fascist groups remain a fringe element, rarely attracting political support in elections, though on occasion they have perpetrated violent acts, most notably a bomb attack on Munich's *Oktoberfest* in 1980, in which thirteen people were killed, and the bombing of Bologna's railway station in the same year, killing eighty-five. Such carnage aside, frankly racist neo-fascist parties have little chance of attracting widespread public support, though "skinhead" adherents of racialist views of course sporadically perpetrate crimes against foreigners, Jews, and immigrants.

It is a measure of the skinhead phenomenon's fringe status these days that despite warnings of racialist attacks on foreigners and immigrants in the German cities hosting the 2006 World Cup—former government spokesman Uwe-Karsten Heye warned non-whites not to enter certain areas because they "might not leave alive"—virtually no such attacks occurred.[48] And when French rightist Jean-Marie Le Pen complained that France's national soccer team, which fields several black and Algerian immigrant players, didn't "look" French, his comments were met with universal condemnation and inspired pre-game anti-racist rituals by the players. Soon after, Le Pen was charged with "complicity in justifying war crimes" for saying in 2005 that in France the "German occupation was not particularly inhumane," which of course it wasn't for the majority of Frenchmen who had no problem coexisting with their occupiers.[49] Le Pen has apparently learned his lesson: black and Arab immigrants figured prominently in his advertisements for the French presidential elections in 2007.[50]

These legal restrictions on comments about the fascist past, as well as informal disapproval of xenophobic sentiments, are another check on a fascist resurgence—at least for now. Yet the spiritual vacuum created by the abandonment of traditional Christianity leaves contemporary Europeans still vulnerable to political religions, including new versions of fascism. Thus, the failure of neo-fascist parties to attract widespread political support on the national level does not mean that core elements of fascism, adapted and repackaged to avoid the taint of racism and the Nazi past, are not a factor in contemporary European politics, where "extreme right" parties have managed in the last two decades to achieve and maintain a political presence in local and central governments.

Over the last twenty years, this support on the national level has hovered on average around 15 percent, with occasional successes beyond that threshold that have attracted media attention and a short-lived influence in national governments.[51] In Austria, Jörg Haider's Freedom Party won 23 percent of the vote in 1994, a share that increased to 27 percent in 1999. In February 2000, Haider's party formed a coalition government with the traditionally dominant People's Party, taking six out of twelve ministerial portfolios. But this success didn't last: by 2004, the Freedom Party's support had shrunk to 6.4 percent. In France, Jean-Marie Le Pen's National Front likewise has only briefly exceeded the 15 percent threshold of voter support, despite a stunning second-place finish in the first round of the 2002 presidential elections. Le Pen's 17 percent share of the vote obviously reflected voter dissatisfaction with Socialist candidate Lionel Jospin rather than solidarity with Le Pen's views; Le Pen garnered only 19 percent of the vote in the runoff with Jacques Chirac. In Italy, the neo-fascist MSI (Movimento Sociale Italiano) renamed itself the Alleanza Nazionale and distanced itself from its fascist roots. Together with the separatist Northern League, the MSI teamed up with Silvio Berlusconi's Forza Italia to win the parliamentary election of 1994. When Forza Italia won again in 2001, Alleanza Nazionale's Gianfranco Fini became vice premier. But by 2006 the Berlusconi alliance was out of power, replaced by the Socialist Eurocrat Romano Prodi.

The failure of far-right parties to break the 15 percent threshold, and the dependence of what success they do achieve on how cleverly they disguise their racist or xenophobic nationalist ideals, does not mean that a fascist revival is not possible. As Paxton points out, in the programs of these parties "one hears echoes of classical fascist themes: fears of decadence and decline; assertion of national and cultural identity; a threat by unassimilable foreigners to national identity and good social order; and the need for greater authority to deal with these problems."[52] These various factors, moreover, converge explosively in the issue of immigration, particularly Muslim immigration. Approximately fifteen to twenty million Muslims now reside in the E.U., many of them warehoused in urban ghettos, chronically unemployed, and over-represented among the criminal class. Their fecundity at the same time that Europeans are aging and not reproducing means that immigration will remain an increasingly disruptive factor in European politics. The European failure to assimilate immigrants, as Timothy Garton Ash notes, may contribute to a "downward spiral which will be the curse of the national politics of Europe for years ahead. Populist, anti-immigrant parties will regularly break through the 15 percent mark in regional and national elections, winning the votes of less affluent native-born voters who resent rapid change in their traditional ways of life and blame immigrants for rising crime and job losses." Immigrant Muslim youth will increasingly become involved in Islamist extremism and outright terrorism, as happened in Madrid and London, thereby reinforcing native-born resentments and fears.[53]

It is not inconceivable that future events will shatter the reserve that at present holds back or disguises more explicit expressions of classic fascist sentiments, and Europe could see a resurgence of violent xenophobia and even racism, particularly as time passes and those responsible for fascism's excesses die off. "The inoculation of most Europeans against the original fascism by its public shaming in 1945 is inherently temporary," Paxton writes. "The taboos of 1945 have inevitably faded with the disappearance of the eyewitness generation. . . . Some future movement that would 'give up free institutions' in order to perform the same functions of mass mobilization for the reunification, purification, and regeneration of some troubled group would undoubtedly call itself something else and draw on fresh symbols. That would not make it any less dangerous."[54]

Another important factor that could fuel a hyper-nationalist revival is the animus against genuine patriotic sentiment that characterizes the jet-setting, "postnational" E.U. elites. This aversion partly reflects the disgust with the excesses bred by fascist mystic nationalism. But it also expresses the pseudo-cosmopolitan doctrines of multiculturalism and its anti-Western prejudices, a topic to which we will return in a later chapter. One measure of this distaste for expressing cultural pride can be seen in the way that scholars who study far-right politics have expanded the concept of "racism" to include cultural chauvinism, a notion, of course, logically incoherent, since the essence of racism is the notion of inherited inferiority, and cultures aren't genetically determined. Elisabeth Carter, for example, finesses the disavowal of biological racism on the part of many far-right parties by speaking of "culturalism" or the "'new' racism," smear terms used to demonize the unexceptional and empirically verifiable notion that in many key respects Western culture is superior to others.[55] The average European is thus made to feel that expressing pride in his national identity and cultural ideals is akin to racism, even as Third World immigrants risk life and limb to abandon their own cultures and come to the West—and, once there, loudly proclaim the superiority of the culture they abandoned and the depravity of the culture that has welcomed them, all the while protected by laws that characterize any criticism of non-Western cultures as a "racism."

This prejudice against open pride in one's own country and culture, often expressed by quoting Samuel Johnson's famous remark that "Patriotism is the last refuge of a scoundrel," does not allow for what James Boswell added to Johnson's statement as an exception: "a real and generous love of our country." The vilification of libertarian Dutch politician Pim Fortuyn—assassinated by an animal-rights activist in 2002—as "racist" and "fascist" and the "Dutch Haider" simply because he publicly expressed concern about the impact of unassimilated Muslim immigrants on Dutch identity, culture, and values, shows how stating one's pride and concern for one's own culture and its integrity instantly marginalizes politicians in Europe.

Yet a "real and generous love of our country" is a natural and important sentiment for creating the shared identity without which a nation disintegrates into a mere aggregate of individuals bound together by nothing more than product consumption and geographical proximity: "Can any nation survive," Michael Burleigh puts the question, "without a consensus on values that transcend special interests, and which are non-negotiable in the sense of 'Here we stand'? Can a nation state survive that is only a legal and political shell, or a 'market state' for discrete ethnic or religious communities that share little by way of common values other than use of the same currency? Can a society survive that is not the object of commitments to its core values or a focus for the fundamental identities of all its members?"[56] Yet any attempt to define and publicize such a consensus often collides with a reflexive charge of racism and xenophobia, as happened in 2000 to Germany's Christian Democrat–Christian Social Union coalition when it attempted to define German culture as part of its platform on immigration policy, and made reference to "Western values."[57]

That many Europeans, contrary to the E.U. overlords, still possess reservoirs of nationalist feeling and cultural pride was evident in the 2006 World Cup soccer tournament, when millions of Europeans cheered hysterically and publicly for their national teams and draped themselves in their nation's flags. Time will tell whether such displays of national affection are the expression of repressed patriotism or its last symbolic gasp. But other evidence suggests that Europeans may be getting tired of the reflexive self-loathing and fashionable guilt that dominate the intellectual class. In March 2004, the French National Assembly passed a bill banning the public display of religious symbols in public schools, a measure clearly targeted at the headscarves (*hijab*) worn by Muslim girls. The veil (*niqab*) and headscarf seem to be a particular locus of European discontent with Muslims: four German states ban public school teachers from wearing *hijab*, Italy has banned the *niqab*, and Britain's former foreign minister Jack Straw ignited a brief firestorm when he spoke out against the veil in October 2006.[58]

Other signs of European impatience with immigrants have been surfacing. In 2005, the French passed a law that requires schoolteachers to emphasize the positive contributions of French colonialism in North Africa, a heretical challenge to the simplistic anti-colonialist orthodoxy that has made the West the villain of history.[59] Even in Sweden, the Netherlands, and Denmark, traditionally some of the most socially inclusive countries in Europe, a *Wall Street Journal Europe* poll found that more than 70 percent of the people thought Muslims were disapproved of. And in Spain, 60 percent say immigration is their country's "principal problem."[60] Such discontent, at present reflected in particular laws and in grass-roots symbolic protests, will increasingly translate into electoral respect for anti-immigrant policies, with more mainstream parties, even on the left, taking tougher stances towards immigrants. This evolution was apparent in the Austrian elections in fall 2006, when the victorious Social Democrats ran on a platform that included cracking down on immigrant crime—while the two far-right parties garnered 15 percent of the vote.[61] And in Amsterdam the same year, the far-right Vlaams Belang party won 20.5 percent of the votes in city elections.

Other, less benign manifestations of nationalist pride can also be gleaned from European popular culture. In Paris, Brussels, and other cities, rightist groups publicly offer "identity soup," made from pork products, as an assertion of European identity pointedly exclusive of Muslims and Jews.[62] Even in Germany, where written laws and informal taboos have made Germans wary of expressing patriotism, race-based national pride percolates below the surface. Nor should we be surprised, for as Claire Berlinski notes, "Profound instincts, when repressed, become sublimated. Like the religious instinct, the instinct to nationalism, when formally denied, will emerge in curious black-market forms."[63] Berlinski's analysis of the lyrics of the German heavy-metal rock group Rammstein, the best-selling band in German history, and her discussion of the symbolism and spectacle of the band's live shows, uncover a German nationalism—what the band calls a "new German hardness"—uncomfortably redolent of Nazi iconography and sensibilities. As one of the band members puts it, Rammstein's music, like Germany's soccer team, "'is about the revival of a *healthy German self-esteem.*" The troubling question is why an assertion of German self-esteem borrows so heavily on a Nazi aesthetic and its "vocabulary, dramaturgy, propaganda, mythology, occultism, death worship, bloodthirstiness, ferocity, nihilism, power-lust, and outrageous sadism."[64] As the years pass and those responsible for the horrors of Nazism die off and the Holocaust retreats into history, younger generations will grow tired of feeling guilty about being German, particularly as German identity comes under increasing assault by unassimilated immigrants. We might see then a wider audience for a "new German hardness."

To many rightists and conservatives, the loss of nationalist pride and the refusal to acknowledge Europe's achievements that characterize the E.U. elite signify the corruption of Western civilization and its decline. Along with the abandonment of Christianity, this indifference to Europe's greatness is blamed for many of the social and political problems facing Europe, from pornography and the acceptance of homosexuality, to the refusal to hold immigrants to European standards and values because of cultural and moral relativism. The focus on Western cultural decline and spiritual depravity has paradoxically provided a rationale for an extreme rightist alliance with radical Islam, for the latter also justifies its assault on the West by focusing on the decay of morals and spiritual impoverishment that has weakened the West and left it vulnerable to a militarily and economically weak but spiritually strong Islam. Preachers of jihad have repeatedly made this point about Western corruption, what Iranian Islamist Al-e Ahmed called "Westoxification." Sayyid Qutb, whose writings have influenced the ideology of modern jihadists, was deeply affected by the time he spent in America, which struck him as a modern Sodom, wholly given over to materialism and pleasure.[65]

This long convergence of interests and enemies on the part of European neo-fascists and Islamic radicals in the future could lead to tactical alliances and collaborative violence as social and economic dysfunction fuels ever more anger and resentment on the part of Europeans and Muslim immigrants alike. The victim, of course, will be the uniquely Western liberal-democratic ideals that the E.U. elite espouse but do very little to strengthen and nurture.

POLITICAL RELIGIONS: GREEN PARTIES

The European Green parties are examples of another "political religion" that, though attracting less electoral support than extreme right parties, has a much greater impact on the larger culture. The support of Green parties across Europe averages around 5 percent, with the exception of Germany and Austria, where support is 3 to 4 percentage points higher.[66] Yet unlike the more electorally successful extreme right parties, the Greens have much more influence over their nation's governments and E.U. politics and policies.

Green parties are at first glance very diverse, from "deep" greens and "shallow" greens to "red" greens (or "watermelons": green on the outside, red on the inside) more closely aligned with the traditional left. Whatever these differences, however, all Greens embrace similar ideas and values that derive from one of the West's most popular pseudo-religions, romantic environmentalism.

Rather than a concern for resource management and protection of the environment, romantic environmentalism is rather a wholesale critique of science, technology, and free-market capitalism. As such, Green ideology is anti-Western at its core. According to Andrew Dobson, the Greens represent a "challenge to the political, social and scientific consensus that has dominated the last two or three hundred years of public life."[67] Part of the Green complaint is directed at the humanistic individualism that characterizes bourgeois society and undergirds modern science: Greens want to "decenter the human being, to question mechanistic science, and to refuse to believe that the world was made for human beings."[68] They believe that selfish individualism, abetted by science, has created consumer capitalism and a material affluence that is not sustainable because it depends on plundering the finite resources of nature and it alienates people from their natural identities.

Like the extreme right parties, Green parties are unhappy with modernity and its consequences, erecting a mythic vision of a more natural human existence ruined by the Enlightenment, industrialism, urbanization, technology, capitalism, and the changes in human life these have wrought: the increased complexity, scale, speed, and psychic discomfort of modern life contrasted with an idealized premodern existence lived more harmoniously with nature. This view of human history, of course, is not factual but mythic. Two myths in particular, the Golden Age myth and the myth of the Noble Savage, both arising with the dawn of complex urban civilizations, express these ideals. Both imagine a simple time before cities and technology, when humans lived in harmony with a maternal earth that provided sustenance for people without the need of work, laws, private property, or complex social institutions. The rise of agriculture marks the "fall" of humanity from this paradise, for it exiled and alienated people from nature and their own more authentic identities, herding them into crowded cities where the old, more cooperative communal mode of life was lost, and law, private property, trade, crime, and greed arose to immiserate mankind—the Iron Age of ancient myth.

Despite romantic environmentalism's frequent recourse to scientific arguments, such ideals and attitudes are not the fruit of rational inquiry or modern science, which tells us that rather than a maternal lost home, nature instead is a harsh world of blind physical forces indifferent to all the life forms created by random mutations and doomed ultimately to extinction. This nature cares nothing for the human-created values the Greens prize, such as peace, justice, beauty, or even a respect for life or "biodiversity." The idealization of primitive societies, who presumably lived in harmony and balance with this mythic nature before the fall into modernity, is also based on myth, for a rational examination of the pain, malnutrition, scarcity, disease, terror, and hard work suffered by our ancestors refutes the Noble Savage notions recycled by modern Greens who have no intention of actually returning to such a presumed paradise.

In short, rather than a statement of reality based on rational thought, romantic environmentalism is a pseudo-religion, a faith complete with a narrative of humanity's fall from grace and a doctrine promising redemption and paradise if only the prophets (Rachel Carson, Barry Commoner, Paul Ehrlich, Al Gore) are heeded and we turn from our wicked ways—that is, capitalism, science, technology, complex urban societies, and particularly globalization—before the apocalypse of environmental degradation destroys humanity and the rest of the planet. Thus, the aim of the Greens is a religious one, "re-creating the spiritual dimension of life that the grubby materialism of the industrial age has torn asunder."[69]

The combination of apocalyptic prophecies and promises of utopia can be found in the "The Charter of the Global Greens," the 2001 statement of Green ideology by the Global Greens, the international network of Green parties and political movements. The core assumption behind this document, what it calls "ecological wisdom," is derived from the old myths of human harmony with nature: "We acknowledge that human beings are part of the natural world and we respect the specific value of all forms of life, including non-human species" (including bacteria, viruses, and cockroaches, I assume). Consistent with this article of a universalistic faith, the rest of the sermon is apocalyptic, predicting disaster for mankind for falling away from this revealed truth: modern science and capitalism are causing "extreme deterioration in the environment and a massive extinction of species." In the Iron Age created by capitalism and science, "injustice, racism, poverty, ignorance, corruption, crime and violence, armed conflict and the search for maximum short-term profit are causing widespread human suffering." To avoid this calamity, Greens must proselytize in order to create "new men": hence the Greens "assert the need for fundamental changes in people's attitudes, values, and ways of producing and living." And the promised redemption that would follow such change is utopian: "Closing the gap between rich and poor and building a citizenship based on equal rights for all individuals in all spheres of social, economic, political and cultural life."[70]

Although much of the ideology underlying the Green political program is as mythic and anti-rational as the ideals of the extreme right, the Greens enjoy much more respectability and have influenced the E.U. program to a degree not reflected in their electoral success. From being totally ignored in earlier E.U. and Common Market policies, these days Green economic policies such as "sustainable development"—a vague and subjective phrase that in practice could mean little or no development at all—has become a "fundamental objective of the European Union," as the Brussels European Council puts it. The accompanying explanation of this E.U. goal incorporates the romantic views of nature typical of the Greens—"Sustainable development is about safeguarding the earth's capacity to support life in all its diversity"—and espouses the trendy utopianism found throughout Green ideology: "democracy, gender equality, solidarity, the rule of law and respect for fundamental rights."[71] Even if these are empty promises, the fact that the E.U. feels compelled to acknowledge the political goals of parties so electorally marginal testifies to the pseudo-religious attraction of Green ideology. Since the economic consequences of pursuing these Green goals would be disastrous, given how fundamentally contrary they are to modern global capitalism and economic development, the fact that even lip service is paid to them suggests that quasi-religious sentiment, not reason and evidence, is behind Green ideology.

Indeed, on nearly every count, the evidence suggests that taking seriously the Green complaints about capitalism and science would be the worst thing for nature and humans, particularly those in the developing world. Contrary to the pronouncements of the anti-globalization lobby, continuing poverty and lack of development represent the most serious threat to the environment. As Jack Hollander, emeritus professor of energy from the University of California at Berkeley, puts it, "Poverty is the environmental villain; poor people are its victims. Impoverished people often do plunder their resources, pollute their environment, and overcrowd their habitats. They do these things not out of willful neglect but only out of the need to survive."[72] Caring for nature is the luxury of those who aren't worried about eating for another day. And free-market capitalism, the villain of the Greens, is the best way to distribute the fruits of prosperity to as many people as possible.

Equally indicative of mythic thinking is the Green opposition to biotechnology, especially genetically modified (GM) foods. In Europe, irrational fears of so-called "Frankenfoods" have lead to the banning or strict controls of GM crops, despite the absence of any evidence that they represent a danger to people or the environment. On the contrary, as the co-discoverer of DNA, James D. Watson, puts it, the "GM plant revolution" has an "astonishing range of potential applications," not just to provide food for billions but to reduce pesticide and herbicide use, thus reducing pollution, and to improve the abundance and nutritional value of food, boons for the impoverished of the Third World.[73] Yet affluent Europeans who take their own nutrition for granted indulge mythic idealizations of nature and anti-capitalism clichés, and they agitate for policies that keep the benefits of biotechnology from those who need it most. Such attitudes make no sense unless one realizes that what we are witnessing is not a rationalist understanding but rather a debased religious one.

The quasi-religious nature of Green politics can be seen clearly in the popularity of José Bové, the son of a French agricultural scientist. Bové has spearheaded protests against globalization and GM foods, becoming famous in 1999 for using his tractor to demolish a McDonald's restaurant in a town near his hometown Larzac. Claire Berlinski, in her analysis of Bové's career, sees him as a modern version of medieval millenarian heretics: he is "the modern prophet of crop worship," preaching a naïve nature-love spiritualism as both a critique of modern civilization and its discontents, and a recipe for a back-to-nature utopia—the same roots of twentieth-century fascism, which likewise touted a utopian future crafted from a mythic past. The more such debased spiritualism influences E.U. policy, as it has in the banning or strict regulations of biogenetic research and GM foods, the more unlikely that solutions will be found for the deprivation and suffering of those in the Third World who, unlike middle-class malcontents like José Bové, do not have the luxury of taking for granted adequate nutrition.

Like the extreme right's, the Greens' ideology is one predicated on hatred of the modern world and a distrust of traditional Christianity. It is no surprise, then, that romantic environmentalism has appeared in the program of some far-right parties, particularly in Germany, where Green support is high compared to the rest of Europe. Indeed, Hitler's Germany was the first modern nation to pass legislation protecting animals and nature: as historian Simon Schama says, "Exterminating millions of lives was not at all incompatible with passionate protection of trees."[74] This same link between ecology and ethnic particularism is evident in contemporary German far-right parties like the Republicans, who call for "preservation of the existence of the German *Volk*, its health and its ecological living-space [*Lebensraum*] as a priority for domestic policy," a goal that will "also foster environmental protection."[75]

From the perspective of such mystic nationalism, the utilitarian, universalizing, materialist thrust of modern civilization is a threat to the unique "essence" of the people and to the natural world as well, particularly the landscape mystically tied to that essence.

Capitalism, radical individualism, and technology are destroying the communal "folk" just as they are destroying nature. Ecologically minded far-right parties thus find in "ethnopluralism," that is, the notion that each unique people is tied to a particular landscape, a much more attractive rationale for xenophobic nationalist sentiment than the old biological racism: "In the New Age milieu of today, with its affinities for ecology, the ultra-right may well find the mystical component it needs to make a truly updated, modernized authoritarian nationalism."[76]

Yet Green politics today resonates much more on the left, which has managed to compensate for communism's failures by highlighting the Marxist critique of industrial capitalism's impact on social life and the environment, while ignoring the unpleasant fact that communist regimes have severely ravaged nature wherever they have taken power even as they failed miserably at providing economic prosperity. That marriage of convenience between the Greens and the traditional left is why at anti-globalization protests the banners of Greenpeace can be seen flying next to the hammer and sickle. Just as communism benefited from the crisis of capitalism in the 1930s, so too today the costs and tradeoffs of globalization offer an opportunity for a communist resurgence, particularly when the critique is made not on the basis of rational argument and empirical evidence, but rather in terms of quasi-religious longings both for redemption from a fallen modern world and for a lost natural paradise.

Despite the Greens' relatively low level of electoral support, romantic environmentalism's ability to appeal to both the left and the right in Europe on the basis of ancient longings and perceived apocalyptic dangers means that this pseudo-religion and its questionable assumptions about humans and their relationship to nature will continue to be a malign force in European politics and economic policy.

DECLINE AND FALL

THE MOLOCH OF POLITICAL RELIGIONS

Communism has been the deadliest of political religions, its toll of between eighty-five and a hundred million dead exceeding by far the fifty million slaughtered by Nazism.[77] Despite this butcher's bill, and despite the gulags, torture, famines, and other oppression associated with communist ideology, there are still European political parties today that proudly call themselves communist. In the last twenty years, such parties rarely have exceeded 10 percent of the vote, doing best in the traditional strongholds of European communism, France and Italy.[78] Yet the European parliamentary system means that, like the Greens and far-right parties, communist parties are still a factor in national elections and policies.

This continuing legitimacy of an ideology more lethal than a universally reviled Nazism cries out for explanation. Martin Amis, in his study of European intellectuals' long romance with communism, contrasts the universal condemnation of Nazism's excesses with the relative indifference to those of Soviet communism: "Everybody knows of Auschwitz and Belsen. Nobody knows of Vorkuta and Solovestky. Everybody knows of Himmler and Eichmann. Nobody knows of Yezhov and Dzerzhinsky. Everybody knows of the six million of the Holocaust. Nobody knows of the six million of the Terror-Famine."[79] Why is the swastika illegal in Europe while the hammer and sickle still waves proudly? Why is Mao's visage an object of camp design while Hitler's is *verboten*? Why are there intellectuals who still loudly proclaim that they are communists while Nazism is a despised fringe cult?

One obvious answer is that communism tapped into the other great, still potent pseudo-religion of modernity: the scientism born of the Enlightenment. In a parody of modern science, communism looks to the future, to reason, to the knowable "laws of history," and believes that progressive improvement of the human condition is the inevitable result of those laws.[80] Nazism, on the other hand, "spat in the face of the Enlightenment," as Orlando Figes puts it, looking to a mythic premodern past to be restored through racial discipline and purifying murder.[81] Communism is universal and proselytizing as well, whereas Nazism and other forms of fascism are particularistic, reserved only for the racial or national group and incompatible with other, lesser races or nations, which must yield to the superior race.[82] Finally, communism shares the materialist determinism of secular modernity: the belief that all causes are material, that humans are mere matter acted upon by the "laws of history" in the same way that nature is subject to the laws of physics. Moreover, knowledge and manipulation of these "laws" on the part of an elite can lead to the transformation of social life to achieve the utopian boons of equality and social justice, since human nature is infinitely malleable and hence through force or indoctrination can be shaped to achieve utopian ends.

Which is another way, of course, of saying that the Marxist theory underlying communism is not "scientific" or the fruit of reason and experience, but rather a pseudo-religion, like positivism and the other manifestations of scientism discussed earlier: "One of the ways," Henri de Lubac says, "in which modern man seeks to escape from any kind of transcendency and to shake off the thing it regards as an unbearable yoke—namely, faith in God."[83] Instead of faith in God, "enlightened" man put his faith in science or pseudo-scientific theories such as positivism, socialism, and communism.

Like the positivists, Marx's socialist predecessors frankly regarded their political and economic ideology as a substitute religion. British spinning-mill magnate Robert Owen, who created the utopian socialist community of New Harmony in Indiana in the 1820s, also started a pseudo-church called by various names, such as the Universal Community Society of Rational Religionists. This creed held Sunday services in "halls of science" where sermons from Owen's works would be read and hymns sung with lyrics such as "Let the claims of *mine* and *thine*/In all-blessing *ours* combine." There were also six paid "socialist bishops" whose calling was to spread the good news. Owen ended up a religious crank, attending séances where he allegedly communed with Benjamin Franklin and Thomas Jefferson.[84]

Karl Marx was famously opposed to any religious faith, asserting that "man makes religion, it is not religion that makes man"; the "State and society," he goes on, "produce religion, a mistaken attitude to the world," an illusion that compensates for man's alienation.[85] He rejected the spiritual and transcendent, reducing all human and social reality to the material. "The production of the immediate material means of subsistence," his collaborator, publicist, and financier Friedrich Engels wrote of Marx's thought, "form[s] the foundation upon which the state institutions, the legal conceptions, art, and even ideas on religion of the people concerned have evolved, and in the light of which they must, therefore, be explained."[86] Thus, Marx fancied himself a "scientist" and empirical rationalist, practicing "the science of real men and their historical development," as Engels put it, and scorning any sort of religion.[87]

The positivists and socialists, however, endorsed the same materialist metaphysic, had the same pretensions to scientific rigor, and were equally opposed to traditional religion— even as they were fabricating their own substitutes. We heard earlier Auguste Comte's assertion that "God has gone, unquestionably and forever," and examined his Religion of Humanity. Likewise, socialist Robert Owen attacked traditional religion, saying that there was no sacrifice that he would not have "willingly and joyously made to terminate the existence of religion on earth."[88] So too Marx, whose philosophy, for all its scorn of irrational faith, ultimately represents not the fruits of reason and experience, but rather the revelation of a pseudo-religion hostile to the traditional faiths that once provided people meaning and value rooted in the transcendent rather than in the material. Thus Marxism, in Michael Burleigh's words, "was a religiously inspired mythopoetic drama carefully camouflaged within various scientific-sounding accretions."[89]

The characterization of communism as a pseudo-religion has been made repeatedly and is indeed something of a cliché, which makes it no less true. The early nineteenth-century socialist Etienne Cabet enthused that "communism is a true religion" and that there is "nothing more essentially religious than communism," an estimation inspired by the model of early Christianity's communal ownership of property.[90] Engels himself noted that socialist meetings "partly resemble church gatherings," as he wrote of one of the Owenite meetings in 1843: "in the gallery a choir accompanied by an orchestra sings social hymns; these consist of semi-religious or wholly religious melodies with communist words."[91]

As a pseudo-religion, Marxist communism indeed borrows much from Christianity, as Michael Burleigh summarizes:

> It is relatively easy to transpose some of the key terms from the Judeo-Christian heritage to Marxism: "consciousness" (soul), "comrades" (faithful), "capitalist" (sinner), "devil" (counter-revolutionary), "proletariat" (chosen people) and "classless society" (paradise). The ruling classes were also going to face a revolutionary form of "Last Judgement" (Welgericht). But there were far deeper unacknowledged correspondences, including nostalgia for a lost oneness and the beliefs that time was linear. . . , that the achievement of higher consciousness brought salvation, and that history was progressing with its meaning and purpose evident to the discerning, knowledgeable vanguard.[92]

These correspondences with, or rather derivations from, Christianity can be fleshed out further. Like Christianity, the Marxist creed is universal, applying to all men everywhere. Just as Christianity sees time and change as providentially ordered toward a transforming culmination, so in Marxism time and change are directed and determined, now by the new god "History," one necessary in a materialist world bereft of the old providential God, yet one just as liberating as the God of Christianity.[93] Communism had its priests, its theologians, and its heretics too—the "deviationists" of so much communist internecine battles and pogroms. And communism had thousands of Torquemadas, the fierce defenders of the faith who, like the Polish communist writer described by Milosz, "hated the enemies of human happiness and insisted that they must be destroyed."[94]

Marx's notion of "alienation," the idea that man under capitalism has been alienated from nature, his fellow man, and especially the fruits of his labor, recalls the Christian notion of the Fall. And just as Christian salvation rescues man from his fallen condition, so too Marxist doctrine offers redemption from alienation, and salvation once private property and capitalism are abolished. Then human nature will be restored, and this earthly paradise "will take away the obsession to have and enable man again to want what as man he ought to want. Senses and perceptions, blinded or stunted in our system, will be released so that again they feel and perceive. Their capacities will be freed. . . ; [m]an again will be natural, an unalienated person in the stream of natural progress," a place "where no discord disturbs the harmonies between man and nature or man and his fellow-man."[95] Chadwick's description of the Marxist utopia strikingly resembles Dante's portrait of the redeemed soul at the end of the *Purgatorio*. As American socialist Michael Harrington wrote of the Marxist utopia, "The sentence decreed in the Garden of Eden will have been served."[96]

The redeemed humanity in Marxist thought recalls the "born-again" Christian: this is the "new man," "the ideal of a liberated, unified humanity that has recovered full possession of its essence, reconciled with itself as with the universe, living in fullness until the consummation of History."[97] But as de Lubac continues, what in Christianity is a spiritual boon is in the Marxist faith an earthly, material paradise in the here and now, beyond necessity and alienation, in which a restored humanity, reaching its highest potential, will no longer need war, exploitation, or oppression. Listen to Leon Trotsky's description of this "new man": "Man will make it his goal . . . to create a higher sociobiological type, a superman. . . . Man will become incomparably stronger, wiser, more subtle. . . . The average human type will rise to the heights of an Aristotle, Goethe, Marx. And beyond this ridge, other peaks will emerge."[98] "Has Christianity," de Lubac asks, "ever asked such an abdication of the mind? On which side are the miracles the most unbelievable?"[99] And let's not forget an important difference with Christianity: the Marxist "new man" will be created by force, if necessary, the "old man" reshaped or destroyed to make way for the new.

Considering how powerfully Marxism combines the old promises of Christianity, now to be realized in this world, with the Enlightenment fantasy of human perfection and social utopia, is it any wonder that this political religion has attracted such passionate devotees? The memoirs of former Marxists consistently use the language of religious conversion to explain their experiences. French author André Gide, writing about his communist beliefs in 1932, said "My conversion is like a faith." The "plan of the Soviet Union seems to me to point to salvation," he continues, and he claims that he would cheerfully martyr himself for this faith.[100] So too Arthur Koestler, who wrote, "I became converted because I was ripe for it and lived in a disintegrating society thirsting for faith," making explicit the link between European secularization and the allure of the communist pseudo-religion. Koestler goes on to describe his conversion in terms that recall St. Paul's on the road to Damascus: "the new light seems to pour from all directions across the skull; the whole universe falls into pattern. . . . There is now an answer to every question, doubt and conflicts are a matter of the tortured past. . . . Nothing henceforth can disturb the convert's inner peace and serenity—except the occasional fear of losing faith again, losing thereby what alone makes life worth living."[101]

Once we see that adherence to Marxism is a consequence of a debased religious thirst for ultimate meaning and value, then the long, stubborn resistance to the historical evidence of Marxism' empirical repudiation and bloody failure becomes more understandable. Then the baffling blindness of generations of what Lenin called "useful idiots," Western apologists for the Soviet Union like H. G. Wells, Sidney and Beatrice Webb, George Bernard Shaw, Jean-Paul Sartre, Lincoln Steffens, Walter Duranty, and many others, is more understandable. Only a religious sensibility can explain the opinion by one of Europe's most famous Marxists, Georg Lukács, that "even if every empirical prediction of Marxism were invalidated, he would still hold Marxism to be true."[102] Like the churchman who refused to look in Galileo's telescope, these true believers preferred to ignore the reality in front of their eyes rather than abandon their faith in something that explained human nature and history and promised paradise on earth, no matter how high the cost in human suffering.

Nor can the failure of Marxism be attributed to a distortion of Marx's ideas by the various regimes that believed they were creating societies consistent with Marx's doctrines. For communists, their creed was always joined to the fate of the Soviet Union: the October Revolution of 1917 was the mythical event that incarnated the Marxist god of History. Throughout the ensuing decades, the allure of communism was intimately tied to the seeming success of the Soviet Union, which financed and encouraged communist parties elsewhere, and whose interests and imperatives communists elsewhere slavishly served and obeyed. Far from being a distortion of communist theory, it is the flawed assumptions behind Marx's theory—the necessary disappearance of private property, and the infinite malleability of human nature, to name two—that ultimately brought down the most powerful nation conceived in its image.[103] Nor did it take the fall of the Soviet Union to bring these flaws to the fore—during Marx's lifetime, the empirical errors and unproven assumptions of his philosophy were apparent. "By the end of the nineteenth century," Robert Conquest writes, "the Marxist predictions of a capitalist failure to expand production, of a fall in the rate of profit, a decrease in wages, of increasing proletarian impoverishment and the resulting approach of revolutionary crisis in the industrial countries had all proved false."[104].

No more believable is the notion that the horrors of Soviet communism were either distortions of Marxism or unknown to people outside of the Soviet Union. Marx in his lifetime endorsed violence and terrorism as justifiable weapons in the revolutionary struggle: "We are ruthless," he threatened the Prussian government in 1843, "and ask no quarter from you. When our turn comes we shall not disguise our terrorism." And the next year, in the "Plan of Action" he distributed in Germany, he wrote, "Far from opposing the so-called excesses, those examples of popular vengeance against hated individuals or public buildings which have acquired hateful memories, we must not only condone these examples but lend them a helping hand."[105] In Marx's view of history, his own generation "must not only conquer a new world, it must also *perish* in order to make room for the people who are fit for a new world."[106]

Nor was Vladimir Lenin the "true" communist whose revolution was hijacked by Stalin, a rationalization first floated by Leon Trotsky and since then used by many communists to salvage their faith from the overwhelming evidence of communism's tyranny and murder. In 1908 Lenin spoke of "real, nation-wide terror, which reinvigorates the country and through which the Great French Revolution achieved glory."[107] True to his beliefs, within a few years after the 1917 revolution, there were in Lenin's Russia "censorship of the press, one-party dictatorship, mass terror, and even concentration camps."[108] Stalin's purges were prefigured by Lenin's war against the "kulaks," the more prosperous peasants: "Merciless war against these kulaks!" he directed, "Death to them." To a cabinet member protesting his decree ordering summary executions, Lenin retorted, "Do you think we can be victors without the most severe revolutionary terror?"[109]

Stalin's famine also had its forerunner in the famine created by Lenin's policies in 1921, when more than five million Russians died. In response to the desperation and chaos he had caused, Lenin saw an opportunity to "usher in socialism." "Famine," a friend reported of Lenin's thinking, "would also destroy faith not only in the tsar, but in God too." Seizing the opportunity, Lenin ordered "the acquisition of [church] valuables with the most ferocious and merciless energy," and demanded "the most decisive and merciless battle to [be given to] the [clergy] and subdue its resistance with such brutality that they will not forget it for decades to come. . . . the greater the number of the representatives of the reactionary bourgeoisie and reactionary clergy that we will manage to execute in this affair, the better."[110] As Richard Pipes concludes, "The despotic powers that Stalin exercised were put in place by Lenin." An old comrade of both dictators, Vyacheslav Molotov, said that Lenin was the more "severe" of the two: "I recall how he scolded Stalin for softness and liberalism."[111]

Finally, communism's failure is confirmed by its own god, History, which is filled with repudiations of Marx's theory and the evidence of the way that theory justified the most horrific excesses. We've already noted the failure of Marxism to anticipate the rising living standards of the proletariat, the willingness of governments to institute social welfare programs to mitigate some of capitalism's costs, and the growth of trade unions and other democratic mechanisms that gave the working class political power, a flaw in the theory pointed out by the first Marxist "deviationist," Eduard Bernstein, at the end of the nineteenth century. World War I was another blow, for the European socialists and working classes ignored their presumed transnational solidarity and went off to fight and die on behalf of their nations. And the Russian Revolution itself "exploded the canonical categories of Marxist doctrine," for it confounded Marxist "scientific" predictions of historical change through clearly defined stages, since communism's first success was not in an advanced industrial nation like Germany with a large proletariat, but in a largely agricultural country.[112]

Worse still, the terror, oppression, and murder extrapolated from Marx's theories first by Lenin and then by Stalin were documented and known right from the start and should have discredited communism in the eyes of any rational observer. The famous philosopher and socialist Bertrand Russell in 1920 wrote about the true nature of Lenin's regime and the misery it was causing the workers it presumed to represent. French true believer Pierre Pascal in 1927 identified one of the core tyrannies of Soviet communism when he wrote in his journal, "No regime has ever been a regime of lies to this extent."[113] Boris Souvarine, another true believer, saw long before Orwell the link between communism and the abuse of language: speaking of the International, the network of communist parties controlled by Moscow, he wrote, "Not one fact, not one quotation, not one idea, not one argument:

only impudent affirmations with a half-dozen interchangeable words come from the 'heights.'"[114] And numerous witnesses tried to tell the world about the oppression and murder and famine in Russia: Panaït Istrati, Ewald Ammende, Otto Schiller, Malcolm Muggeridge, Karl Kautsky, André Gide, Victor Serge, and Ante Ciliga, to name the lesser-known. "Those who wanted to know could have known," François Furet writes. "The problem was that few people really wanted to."[115] Communism was too powerful a faith to be weakened by reality. And this fervent belief persisted, surviving Stalin's betrayal of the Spanish left, his collusion with Hitler, the enslavement of Eastern Europe, the crushing of democracy in Prague and Budapest and Berlin and Warsaw—indeed, all throughout the Cold War up until the very moment the Soviet Union, communism's most important incarnation of Marx's theory, imploded.

And not even that dramatic repudiation by History has weakened the hold that this pseudo-religion still has over many people today, especially in Europe. Harvey Klehr and John Earl Haynes are two of the first scholars to study the Soviet archives opened by Russian president Boris Yeltsin in 1992, and their research documented Soviet communism's expansive ambitions for world domination and its active subversion of Western liberal democracies, motives long derided as anti-communist hysteria by devoted Western communists and fellow travelers. "Communism as a social fact is dead," they write. "But communism as a pleasant figment of the 'progressive' world view lives on, giving a phantom life to the illusions and historical distortions that sustained that murderous and oppressive ideology."[116]

And that is why detailing the failures of communism is still important, for the underlying beliefs that animated it—that social and human reality are to be explained by material causes, that an elite of technicians knowledgeable of those causes and armed with state power can reshape human nature and create utopian boons such as equality, and that free-market capitalism is inherently evil—these beliefs are still powerful today, particularly in Europe. They underlie socialist ideals, which many believe are still viable, despite the demise of exclusively socialist parties. And they provide the core assumptions behind the policies of the E.U.

The lingering effects of these socialistic assumptions are evident in expensive social-welfare entitlements, and in government and E.U. interference in the economy. We've already mentioned the extensive and expensive government-funded entitlements typical of Europe: cradle-to-grave health care, generous unemployment and retirement benefits, short workweeks and work years, and numerous other government transfers designed to cushion the citizen from the slings and arrows of human existence. But all these expensive entitlements cost money. In the three largest continental European economies, France, Germany, and Italy, social welfare spending averages 27 percent, and government spending as a percentage of Gross Domestic Product (GDP) averages over 50 percent, compared to 17 percent and 36 percent in the U.S.[117] Moreover, such transfers of wealth depend on tax receipts that in turn depend on an expanding economy and workforce. European economies, however, have not been performing as well as Asian and American ones, partly because of high tax rates, intrusive regulation on economic activity, government ownership of some key businesses, and numerous disincentives to the entrepreneurial spirit driving economic growth in the rest of the world.

The result of Europe's combination of social welfare spending and government interference in the market is low growth, chronic unemployment, and economic stagnation, as evident in the statistical data. Over the last twenty-eight years, GDP has grown 2.3 percent in the E.U., versus 3.2 percent in the U.S. The United States' purchasing power is 7.6 times GDP, the E.U.'s 6.6. The

GDP per capita in the E.U. is 31 percent less than in the U.S., a proportion unchanged since 1970. If this disparity persists, according to the Organization for Economic Co-operation and Development, in twenty years the average American will be twice as rich as the average Frenchman or German. Employment growth rate in the E.U. is 0.55 percent, in the U.S. 1.62 percent. In the U.S. 74 percent of working-age people are employed, in the E.U. 66 percent; but this figure does not take into account that many European jobs are in government or are state-subsidized. While unemployment rates as of August 2006 were 4.7 percent in the U.S., in the Eurozone they were 7.9 percent: 8.8 percent in France, 8.5 percent in Germany, and 7.4 percent (March 2006) in Italy, the three biggest continental E.U. economies.[118] In category after category—productivity, worker-friendly requirements for wages and fringe benefits, regulations concerning hiring and firing, spending on research and development and education, investment in computers and telecommunications-the E.U. lags behind the U.S.[119]

Nor are these problems merely technical, to be solved by new policies or new laws. They reflect instead deep-seated assumptions about the responsibilities of the state in improving people's lives, assumptions whose roots lie in socialist ideals such as full equality. "The attitude still most widely held in Europe," Olaf Gersemann writes, "is that it is the job of politicians to distribute and redistribute society's goods—be it jobs, income, or wealth. There is a deep zero-sum mentality in Europe which starts from the idea that politics, not competition, should govern economies."[120] Animated by such utopian socialist goals, Europeans cannot accept the short-term tradeoffs and costs that lead to long-term economic health.

In March 2006, massive protests by 2.7 million French against a minor loosening of firing restrictions for entry-level workers starkly illustrated the deep-seated utopian expectations among many Europeans that they should be insulated against economic risk and discomfort. The law was quite modest: employees would serve a two-year trial period, during which they could be more easily let go. The new regulation was specifically designed to ease unemployment among young people, which averages 23 percent. Yet those same young people—three-quarters of whom want to become civil servants with a job for life—rioted against the changes, ultimately dooming them. On the same day in England, hundreds of thousands of public-sector workers went on strike to protest government plans to eliminate for *some* public workers the so-called "rule of 85," which allows public workers to retire at full benefits at age 60 if they have 25 years of service—an unsustainable burden on taxpayers.

Behind these self-defeating attitudes in both countries lie old socialist and communist ideals of absolute economic equality and security—as Robert Leiken reported of the signs carried by the overwhelmingly leftist marchers in Paris, "Causes and ideas that were young in nineteenth-century Europe had escaped from their nursing homes in Pyongyang, Havana, and Minsk."[121]

These socialist attitudes underlying the government policies that strangle European economies comprise the most dangerous legacy of the communist pseudo-religion. The notion that, as Europhile T. R. Reid puts it approvingly, "the state has a responsibility to insulate and protect people from the harsh vicissitudes of modern life" and that people "need to be taken care of by the government and not left alone to bear the consequences of ill fate or their own bad decisions," when put into practice infantilizes people and erodes their autonomy and self-reliance.[122] A Pew poll in 2004 found that twice as many Europeans as Americans agreed that "success is determined by forces outside our control."[123] At the same time, the idea that the state has a responsibility to create equality and happiness for people expands and empowers the government elites who keep the whole therapeutic machinery going. Such elites will necessarily be anti-democratic, and their activities will necessarily limit individual freedom, as Alexis de Tocqueville understood as early as 1848: "Democracy extends the sphere of individual freedom, socialism restricts it. Democracy attaches all possible value to each man; socialism makes each man a mere agent, a mere number. Democracy and socialism have nothing in common but one word: equality. But notice the difference: while democracy seeks equality in liberty, socialism seeks equality in restraint and servitude."[124] This demand for absolute equality of result and security from the risks of freedom paves the "road to serfdom" so brilliantly analyzed by F. A. Hayek.

Some may argue that such socialism has been discredited. But Europe's economic sclerosis brought on by government interference in the market, and its social welfare extravagance both suggest that socialist assumptions are still powerful, as does the continuing animus against the free-market capitalism that has underwritten the E.U. paradise. In a world where growing economic powerhouses like China and India have enthusiastically embraced free-market economies, these old utopian ideals are a recipe for continuing decline.

Apart from these economic consequences, the persistence of communist and socialist ideas reinforces a dangerous self-loathing among many Westerners, what Pope Benedict XVI has called "a peculiar Western self-hatred that is nothing short of pathological."[125] The formula that accounts for the West's success in bringing material prosperity and individual freedom to large numbers of people—free-market capitalism and liberal democracy—is anathema to the socialistic sensibility, intoxicated as it is with the utopian dream of absolute equality brought about by government planning and technocratic control. Thus, the European communist parties have insinuated themselves into the anti-globalization movement, for whatever weakens and discredits this formula provides an opportunity for a return to the old, discredited ideals of communism.

Worse, these anti-Western Western leftists function as a fifth column for the jihadist enemies of the West. The Islamic jihadists have been adept at finding allies among leftists who hate their own culture as much as the jihadists do. Particularly in England, Melanie Phillips reports, "Islamic jihad has turned into the armed wing of the British left." London's far-left mayor, Ken Livingstone, has made a marriage of convenience with radical Islam, publicly and enthusiastically embracing Sheikh Yusuf al-Qaradawi, the Muslim Brotherhood leader who has endorsed the terrorist murder of Jews, which didn't stop Livingstone from comparing him to Pope John XXIII. The buffoonish former Labour M.P. George Galloway likewise found an alliance with radical Islam conducive to furthering both his leftist aims and his own career. The Muslim Association of Britain, part of the jihadist Muslim Brotherhood, has joined with the Socialist Workers Party and the Communist Party of Britain in a coalition to protest the war in Iraq.[126] Despite Islam's contempt for everything the left presumably stands for, radical Islam's hatred of the West makes the jihadists suitable allies for a political ideology that despite being discredited by the success of its most bitter enemy, still retains a powerful, quasi-religious hold on its believers.

THE WAGES OF DISBELIEF

All the pseudo-religions discussed above contribute to the erosion of belief in the Western way, for they all to varying degrees stand opposed to the core values that made the West the dominant civilization on the planet: the dignity of the individual, free-market capitalism, and liberal democracy, all of which derive in large part from Christianity. Secularization's attack on Christianity, then, has severed European culture from its roots, from the very ideals that created the West in the first place. Shorn of transcendent validation, the ideals that Europeans profess—equality, tolerance, democracy, human rights—are now just culturally contingent alternatives that must compete against other visions of the human good, such as Islam, that *do* claim transcendent authority.

Without that authority, moreover, the West's ideals cannot compel people to die and kill to defend them, for people will no longer passionately believe that these ideals are the best way to live, nor will they have the resources for resisting other ways much more oppressive and inhuman. George Orwell, who approved of this process of secularization, was nonetheless honest enough to see its malign consequences: "For two hundred years," he wrote in 1940, "we had sawed and sawed and sawed at the branch we were sitting on. And in the end, much more suddenly than anyone had foreseen, our efforts were rewarded, and down we came. But unfortunately there had been a little mistake. The thing at the bottom was not a bed of roses after all, it was a cesspool full of barbed wire."[127]

Yet many Europeans still want to endorse and enjoy the benefits of the values they no longer will defend: they are what Spanish poet Miguel de Unamuno over eighty years ago called "spiritual parasites," living off Christian ideals without contributing anything to keeping the host alive.[128] And that means the "parasite" will eventually die along with the "host," for as Christopher Dawson writes, "Where unifying spiritual vision is lost—where it is no longer transmitted to the community as a whole—the civilization decays."[129]

The loss of Christian faith has exacerbated other tendencies within Western culture that further weaken its response to the challenge of Islamic jihad. The reduction of all human reality to the material, the assumption that underlies the scientific secular vision, impoverishes human nature, leaving us all nothing more than the sum of our pleasures, and removing any reason why we should care about anything over than our own comfort and security. For, as theologian Michael Novak writes, "Unless human beings have a vision of something larger than their own natures, and beyond the bounds of their own natures, they cannot be pulled out of themselves; they cannot be inspired; and they will not *aspire*, in the way that Gothic steeples aspire. . . . *Real* transcendence is from outside, a new form of life, a new human nature, an uplifting into participation in the divine."[130] Without that "unifying spiritual vision" Dawson speaks of, people no longer form a true community that can collectively strive and create and improve—or defend itself against its enemies.

Next, the loss of transcendence creates the sickness of moral relativism, the notion that, as Hamlet put it, "Nothing's good or bad, but thinking makes it so." Without a passionate conviction in the absolute reality of good and evil, Western man becomes paralyzed, and like Hamlet finds it difficult to act, for the bases of action always involve negotiable material goods and innumerable, uncertain physical causes. "Relativism has wreaked havoc," Pope Benedict XVI writes, "and it continues to act as a mirror and an echo chamber for the dark mood that has fallen over the West. It has paralyzed the West, when it is already disoriented and at a standstill, rendered it defenseless when it is already acquiescent, and confused it when it is already reluctant to rise to the challenge."[131] Cultural relativism exacerbates this paralysis, for its doctrine that all cultures are equally good is empirically false—as proven by the one-way direction of immigration from the non-West to the West, and by the non-West's imitation of the West—and makes it impossible to pass judgment on dysfunctional cultures and to stand up for the unique good of one's own when it is under attack.

Finally, the Enlightenment notion that lies behind most of the pseudo-religions still vexing the West—that reason and technique wielded by experts can create "new men" and usher in the utopia of justice, happiness, and equality-is false to human nature and experience. The Christian understanding of the human predicament is closer to the mark: we are fallen creatures who will never achieve perfection in this world, and so we must always acknowledge the non-negotiable limits of our abilities and the constants of our experience. Pain, suffering, failure, and loss are not anomalies to be engineered from human life, but rather the defining and ennobling conditions of what we are and what makes us great. This tragic vision of human life accepts that utopia is literally "nowhere," and that, as Kant put it, "From the crooked timber of humanity nothing straight can be made." The therapeutic vision underlying modernity's most pernicious pseudo-religions believes instead that perfection is possible, and that the manipulation of the laws of nature and society by enlightened elites can create utopia and happiness for all. This same vision animates much of the E.U. program and the social welfare and economic policies of European governments. As such, it is a dangerous illusion, and false to the complexity of human reality, as the utopian-driven disasters of the previous century attest.

The consequences of Europe's loss of certainty and confidence are evident in the most dramatic fact revealing Europe's suicidal death wish: the disappearance of Europe's children. The demographic data are stark: Europeans are no longer reproducing at the replacement rate of 2.1 children per woman, which means that more people are dying than are being born. In 2000, the E.U. fertility rate was 1.5, ranging from 1.2 in Spain and Italy to 1.4 in Germany and 1.7 in France, the latter rate reflecting the fertility of immigrants. Eurostat, the statistical office of the European communities, calculates that by 2050 the E.U. population, even after increasing via immigration, will have seven million fewer people than in 2004.[132] According to projections by *The Economist* magazine, Europe's median age then will be nearly fifty-three years, compared to nearly thirty-eight in 2002. This means that by 2050, 60 percent of Europe's citizens could be retired and collecting state pensions.[133]

The impact of this sustained loss of people will create conditions usually seen in history after plagues and massacres. Germany will lose the equivalent of the entire population of East Germany. In Italy, 42 percent of Italians will be over sixty, and 60 percent will be without brothers, sisters, cousins, aunts, and uncles.[134] In Spain, the population is halving with every generation.[135] And what few people are left will be old: the proportion of people over sixty-five will double in the E.U., and Europe will lose fifty-two million working-age people.[136] It won't be long before all of Europe resembles Genoa today: "Children are no longer playing in the streets here. . . . Schools have closed for lack of students. Hospitals are overburdened with the elderly. Medical costs are straining the government."[137] The impact of a graying population, a shrinking workforce—by 2050, there will be seventy-five pensioners for every hundred workers[138]—and expensive pensions and health care entitlements "could be very severe for the E.U.'s future growth," Guillermo de la Dehesa writes. "A graying population means a less active population, less entrepreneurship, less innovation, higher and probably unsustainable public expenditures, all of which will result in lower growth."[139] The E.U. *dolce vita* paradise, in other words, is doomed because Europeans will not create the one thing necessary for cultural vigor and economic growth—human capital.

The causes of this demographic disaster, of course, are complex, but as George Weigel argues, the collapse of faith has contributed to the unwillingness of Europeans to see beyond the present and their own comfort and pleasure. "The failure to create a human future in the most elemental sense—by creating a successor generation—is surely an expression of a broader failure: a failure of self-confidence. That broader failure is no less surely tied to a collapse of faith in the God of the Bible."[140] People of faith tend to have larger families because the divine command to "be fruitful and multiply" is more important than the high cost of bearing and raising children.[141] Faith provides the confidence that if we obey God, we will have a future to pass on to our children. Thus, if we believe that the way we live is not just the best way, but one sanctioned by divine authority; and if we believe that "Man does not live by bread alone," that obedience to God, not material pleasures and goods, is the *summum bonum* of human destiny, then we will have confidence in the future of our civilization as something greater than our mortal bodies and create those who will inherit it from us after we have died. But if we believe, like the secularists, that the way we live is no better or worse than any other, that our values are accidents of history or environment, and that the material comforts and pleasures of the present are the highest goods, then we will care nothing for the future of our civilization, and instead we will devote our time and resources to gratifying our own wishes and desires and insuring our own comfort and leisure.

Meanwhile, in Europe there are fifteen to twenty million Muslims who are younger, more prolific, and more confident in their way of life and its sanction by the divine than are the graying Europeans whom many Muslims see as decadent and weak precisely because they ground their lives in material comfort and pleasure rather than in faith. "Islam has youth and will," Mark Steyn writes, "Europe has age and welfare."[142] Fired with spiritual certainty, filled with hatred for the godless West, abandoned by a European society that, riven with doubt about the goodness and rightness of its own culture, has not required (or frequently not allowed) immigrants to assimilate to Western values and norms, radicalized European Muslims are the Morlocks destined to devour an exhausted civilization.

THREE

■■■■■

EURABIA

SUICIDE BY IMMIGRATION

IN 1973, French travel writer Jean Raspail published *The Camp of the Saints*, a disturbing yet prophetic novel about the impact of immigration on European civilization. Raspail's parable turns on a simple yet powerful plot device: beginning in India, then continuing throughout the Third World, millions of impoverished people hijack ships and begin to sail en masse to Europe. Raspail's story follows the first flotilla, from India, as it makes its way to the south of France. Once there, its passengers swarm onto the Côte d'Azur while the French flee in panic to the north. But perhaps the most prophetic part of the story is Raspail's description of the response of Europe to this invasion: a complete capitulation and betrayal of Western civilization in the face of its own demise—in other words, an act of suicide.

This suicidal response to the invasion reveals all the cultural toxins that have infected the West since World War II. The fashionable self-loathing guilt over supposed Western crimes like racism, imperialism, and colonialism both weakens the Europeans and emboldens the invaders. In the novel, the French consul in India, chastising the Catholic bishop who approves of the mass migration and is proud to be "bearing witness," retorts, "Bearing wit-

ness to what? To your faith? Your religion? To your Christian civilization? Oh no, none of that! Bearing witness against yourselves,
like the anti-Western cynics you've become. Do you think the poor
devils that flock to your side aren't any the wiser? Nonsense! They
see right through you. For them, white skin means weak convictions. They know how weak yours are, they know you've given
in." Raspail shrewdly links the Western failure of nerve in the face
of existential assault to the decline of Christian faith: "Who
knows," the narrator writes after Europe has been lost, "how things
might have worked out if the peoples of the West, in similar
straits, had put their faith in God." For in the conflict between
two radically different cultures, "One still believes. One doesn't.
The one that still has faith will move mountains. That's the side
that will win. Deadly doubt has destroyed all incentive in the
other. That's the side that will lose."[1]

Over the past quarter-century, Raspail's dark vision of Europe's
future has come closer and closer to reality. Flotillas of illegal
immigrants regularly cross the Mediterranean from North Africa,
ten thousand having made it to the Italian islands of Lampedusa
and Pantelleria. And now boats are setting out from more distant
Senegal—in 2006, thirty thousand Senegalese and other Africans
landed in the Canary Islands, most hoping to settle in Spain, which
in recent years has received four million new immigrants. Once
there, even illegal immigrants can have access to health care and
other social services, not to mention an open door to the rest of
E.U. Europe.[2] Yet these incursions represent merely a fraction of
the mainly Muslim immigrants who for the past several decades
have, whether legally or not, poured into Europe.

They came first as temporary workers, many from the most
underdeveloped regions of their home countries, who never went
home and then brought their families to Europe under "family
reunification programs." Then there were the "asylum seekers" and

"political refugees," presumed victims of political oppression who very frequently were merely economic migrants. They simply tore up their identification papers on the plane: "A simple ruse," Bruce Bawer writes, "that enables them to avoid deportation and secure residency on humanitarian grounds."[3] Worse yet, in 1989 the European Convention on Human Rights prohibiting torture and degrading treatment was broadened so much that illegal immigrants could not be deported to any country where they could potentially be abused in such fashion. Similarly, in England the definition of a refugee was expanded to cover just about anyone who could argue he might face harm in his own country.[4] These laws made it difficult to control immigration and deport undesirables. But more than anything, the way European governments have treated immigrants once they reach Europe —an incoherent combination of indulgent appeasement and cruel neglect—has created the simmering problem that with every passing day makes Raspail's parable eerily prescient.

Europe's conflicting treatment of its immigrants is summarized by Kathleen Newland of the Migration Policy Institute: "America protects its welfare system from immigrants but leaves its labour markets open, while the E.U. protects its labour markets and leaves its welfare system open."[5] Poorly performing economies, burdensome hiring and firing restrictions, lack of economic mobility, and residual prejudice close immigrants and their children off from honest work and the boons that follow. The result is unemployment rates for second- and third-generation Muslims over twice that of the native-born. In France, which in November 2005 suffered six nights of rioting and thousands of cars burned by the children of Muslim immigrants, the unemployment rate is 40 percent, four times the national average.[6] In England, the unemployment rate of Muslims is three times higher than that of other groups.[7] Compared to the United States, where immigrants are roughly equal contributors to the nation's prosperity, Europe's sluggish economies and overregulated hiring practices prevent immigrants from contributing to the prosperity of their new homes. One study of Denmark's labor force found the gap between native-born and immigrant contributions to the economy to be 41 percent.[8]

If the lack of employment opportunities isn't bad enough, Europe lavishes welfare benefits on immigrants, a surefire formula for creating a sullen, unproductive underclass herded into segregated enclaves like the *banlieues* of Paris or the "dish cities" of Amsterdam, a reference to the television satellite dishes covering the rooftops. When immigrants arrive in England, Roger Scruton writes, they find a "red carpet of legal privileges, eagerly unrolled by publicly funded lawyers, and . . . a welcome trough of welfare benefits that few indigenous citizens can claim."[9] Nor does Scruton exaggerate: the four Muslims who carried out the 2005 terrorist bombings in London had received half a million pounds of taxpayer money. In Norway, immigrants receive a whole panoply of benefits, including welfare, cash payments, disability payments, rent allowance, and a driver's license that costs a native-born Norwegian around $2,000. Such generosity means that immigrants not only do not contribute to their host country's economy at a rate comparable to the native-born, but also take from the economy at a much higher rate. In Denmark, Muslims immigrants make up 5 percent of the population but receive 40 percent of welfare outlays.[10]

The restrictive citizenship policies of many European countries —the probationary period in Italy is ten years, with numerous hard-to-meet requirements—and the impermeability of privileged governmental and educational institutions partially account for the failure of Muslim immigrants to assimilate as smoothly and successfully as they have in the United States, a disability, of course, passed on to their children. In England, only two members of Parliament are Muslim, even though representation proportionate to their population would give Muslims twenty: "Muslims are similarly underrepresented," Claire Berlinski writes, "in the senior ranks of the civil service, prison service, police force, criminal justice system, and armed forces." In France, not a single Muslim sits in the Chamber of Deputies, despite Muslims comprising roughly 10 percent of the population, and only a few of France's thirty-six thousand mayors are immigrants.[11] Higher education is no more accessible. The *grandes écoles* of France, frankly elitist in their admission policies, are the passport to power and privilege in government and business. Yet given that they recruit from fewer than fifty preparatory schools—usually located in the wealthiest neighborhoods and thus seldom attended by immigrants—the latter are effectively barred from this avenue to success.[12]

Unsurprisingly, in many European countries immigrants and their children, the majority Muslim, are overrepresented among those committing crimes and doing time. In Germany, for example, a third of prisoners are foreigners, while only 9 percent of the population is.[13] Prisoners in France are nine times more likely to have North African fathers than French ones.[14] In Sweden, immigrants are four times more likely to be suspected of violent crimes and robbery, and five times more likely to be investigated for sexual assault. A survey of ninth-grade boys in Rinkeby, a Muslim suburb of Stockholm, confirmed these data: 17 percent had forced someone to have sex, and 31 percent had assaulted someone so badly that the victim required medical care.[15] In the Dutch city of Amersfoort, Bruce Bawer reports, "the police have files on 21 percent of local Moroccan boys and 27 percent of Somali boys, and suspect that 40 percent of the Moroccans between age fifteen and seventeen are involved in crime."[16] Then there are the crimes, particularly against women, justified by Islamic doctrine or

home-country custom: honor killings, wife beating, forced marriages of underage girls, and genital mutilation.

The Paris car-burning riots of November 2005, sparked by the
death of two young men electrocuted while hiding from the police,
graphically illustrated just how out-of-control immigrant crime
is in some parts of Europe. The unemployed second-generation
Muslim immigrants festering in the *banlieues*, the ugly public
housing projects surrounding many French cities, inhabit a "kind
of anti-society," essayist Theodore Dalrymple writes, "a population that derives the meaning of its life from the hatred it bears for
the other, 'official' society in France." These neighborhoods are
filled with obscene graffiti, hate-filled rap music, and the hulks of
burned-out cars. Police only rarely dare to enter the more than eight
hundred "sensitive areas" surrounding French cities and known
collectively as *la Zone.* [17]

The thousands of cars burned in 2005, along with widespread
looting, arson, assaults, and vandalism, not to mention the twenty-
five hundred wounded police officers, were a more concentrated
and visible manifestation of the daily disorder that characterizes
the immigrant ghettos of French cities but rarely makes the international news. Even as Paris was burning, in the cathedral town of
Evreux in Normandy, two hundred immigrant "youths," as they
are delicately called, went on a rampage armed with baseball bats,
destroying a shopping mall, a post office, two schools, fifty vehicles,
and the police station. As for burning cars, even before the riots
of November, twenty thousand cars had been torched in France
that year. Nor did all the coverage of the November riots and subsequent influx of government money lead to any reduction in
crime. In the first half of 2006, according to French police, violent
robberies increased 23 percent and assaults 14 percent; across all
of France, there were four hundred eighty violent assaults on
police. [18] During the March 2006 protests in Paris against revising

hiring and firing laws, the so-called *casseurs*, or "smashers," comprising mostly immigrant Muslim youth, infiltrated the marches and smashed shop windows, beat and robbed passersby, and set cars on fire. In October 2006, four violent assaults of police officers by gangs of immigrant youths occurred in the Muslim enclave of Épinay-sur-Seine. Buses were firebombed, and in Marseille, a young woman, herself an immigrant, was set on fire. As Bruce Bawer reports, such violence is a regular occurrence across Europe.[19]

The United States, of course, has its own problems with illegal immigrants, who in some states are overrepresented among criminals and prison inmates. But there are critical differences between immigrants in the United States and those in Europe. As a country shaped by immigration from the beginning, the U.S. has had centuries of experience in assimilating newcomers. We lack a tradition of mystic exclusionary nationalism, and attempts to enforce such "blood and soil" notions have always end up failing in the face of America's regional, religious, and ethnic diversity. Equally important, as noted earlier, our economy is much more open and welcoming, much more accommodating to entrepreneurs, much more rich in economic opportunity than are E.U. economies. And most important, the bulk of our immigrants, especially illegal ones, come from countries like Mexico whose cultures are essentially Western and Christian, and they arrive in a country more welcoming to the practice of faith. Consequently, immigration in America is a mainstream issue easily, if contentiously, discussed in the public square. In Europe, on the other hand, the topic of immigration has been associated with the extreme right and thus tainted as racist. Indeed, in England the uproar over conservative politician Enoch Powell's famous, and increasingly prescient, 1968 "Rivers of Blood" speech about the dangers of unrestricted immigration, cost Powell his political career and made it impossible to discuss immigration for decades.

In contrast to American immigrants, Muslim immigrants to Europe and their children are much different from the people of their host countries. Islam historically has been exclusionary and chauvinistic, brooking no deviation from the truth revealed to Muhammad, "seal of the prophets." Thus, for many Muslim immigrants, their primary loyalty is to Islam and its religious laws, not to the laws or customs of their new home. And Islamic doctrine legitimizes violence in defense of the faith and in pursuit of Allah's injunction to "fight all men until they say, 'There is no god but Allah,'" as Muhammad put it in his farewell address. This spiritual intolerance makes it harder to assimilate with a secularized European culture that views faith as a quaint holdover from more primitive times.

Core Islamic beliefs such as the subordination and sequestration of women, and a disdain for homosexuality and sexual excess, daily collide with a hedonistic popular culture of sexual license and hostility to religion. Writing of Amsterdam's red-light district, where every form of sexual perversion is advertised on the street by "window prostitutes," Dutch essayist Ian Buruma wonders if "such a naked display of man's animal instincts could be seen as a form of barbarism," one that is an "intolerable provocation" for people of faith.[20] Nor does it help when the Dutch answer to the problem of assimilation is to show newcomers a DVD depicting topless women and two men kissing. As for the true culture of the West, how can it be presented as an attractive alternative and its unique goods celebrated when its public face is one of decadence and trivial pleasure, and when its own intellectuals are eager to voice their hatred of its achievements? Combine all these ingredients, and you have a poisonous brew for creating terrorists like those who bombed London and Madrid, most of whom were citizens of the countries they attacked, unlike the 9/11 terrorists, none of whom were U.S. citizens.

Moreover, the materialist determinism of the West that has filled the vacuum created by the decline of faith is particularly useless for addressing the spiritual conflicts at the root of immigrant discontent, for Muslim cultural and religious prejudices are more important than a lack of economic or educational opportunity. The therapeutic superstition that destructive behavior should not be judged or punished, but rather "cured" with counseling, jobs programs, recreation centers, and other social-welfare transfers does nothing but create contempt among those such measures are supposed to help: "The *laxisme* of the French criminal justice system," Dalrymple writes, " is now notorious. Judges often make remarks indicating their sympathy for the criminals they are trying (based upon the usual generalizations about how society, not the criminal, is to blame)."[21] This laxity explains why after the 2005 riots in France, only one of the eighty-five young men who were arrested during the riots was in jail.[22] Instead of punishment, as Mark Steyn reports, the government promoted a "'raft of measures'—the creation of an anti-discrimination agency, twenty thousand job contracts with local government agencies, an extra 100 million euros for community associations." But the true emblem of Western moral bankruptcy was not so much the government blood money but rather the monument constructed in honor of the two youths whose accidental deaths while evading the police sparked the riots.[23] Of course, no such recognition was granted to the thousands of police officers injured while attempting to protect the public. Such appeasement only convinces the jihadists that their estimation of the West's spiritual weakness is correct, and that the holy war can ultimately prevail.

Theodore Dalrymple has shrewdly analyzed this potent mix of traditional Islamic prejudice with Western cultural decadence, one creating a "potential space" for Islamic radicalism and "its ready-made diagnosis and prescriptions," a space filled with "the pus of implacable hatred for many in search of a reason for and a solution to their discontents." Schooled by generations of Western artists and academics in the evils of the West, a condemnation reinforcing traditional Islamic disdain for the "infidel," many Muslims believe that "the West can never meet the demands of justice, because it is decadent, materialistic, individualistic, heathen, and democratic rather than theocratic. Only a return to the principles and practices of seventh-century Arabia will resolve all personal and political problems at the same time." Of course, for Muslim immigrant children, their attraction to Western popular culture, freedom, pleasure, and material affluence creates a division within their souls, leaving them riven with guilt and doubt. But this wound can be spectacularly healed through martyrdom in the path of jihad: "By means of suicide bombing," Dalrymple concludes, "the bombers overcome moral impurities and religious doubts within themselves and, supposedly, strike an external blow for the propagation of the faith."[24]

Yet in the face of this threat, Europe for the most part has chosen the road of appeasement, like the Europeans of Raspail's novel seemingly content to watch their magnificent civilization evolve into Eurabia, a culture in which Islam and its religious law, *sharia*, will more and more displace the Judeo-Christian and classical goods of the West—individual rights and autonomy, democracy, independent thought, everything that has delivered freedom and prosperity to millions of people. How did this slow-motion suicide happen?

CREATING EURABIA

Eurabia was a journal published in the mid-1970s by the European Committee for Coordination of Friendship Associations with the Arab World. That title has been borrowed by scholar Bat

Ye'or to describe "Europe's evolution from a Judeo-Christian civilization, with important post-Enlightenment secular elements, into a post-Judeo-Christian civilization that is subservient to the ideology of *jihad* and the Islamic powers that propagate it." The result is that Europe is turning into Eurabia— a "civilization of dhimmitude," content to sacrifice Israel today, and its own cultural identity in the future, for temporary peace of mind and economic benefits.

Ye'or has written in depth on the mentality of Islamic jihad and its corollary dhimmitude, her term for the condition of *dhimmi*, the "subjugated, non-Muslim individuals or people that accept the restrictive and humiliating subordination to an ascendant Islamic power to avoid enslavement or death," a subordination that included paying the *jizya*, the poll tax.[25] Starting in the mid-twentieth century, Ye'or argues, jihad has returned as a force in the Muslim world. Yet pursuing jihad through war, as in the past, is fruitless in the face of Western economic and military dominance. Thus, political, economic, and psychological weapons, particularly the violence of terrorism, constitute the jihad by other means.

In her exhaustive study *Eurabia*, Ye'or documents both the jihad by other means that the Arab states have waged against its traditional enemy, and the craven appeasement with which the European political elite has faced a threat that their ancestors met and turned back at Poitiers, Andalusia, Lepanto, and Vienna. In contrast to its ancestors, "Europe, as reflected by the institutions of the E.U., has abandoned resistance for dhimmitude, and independence for integration with the Islamic world of North Africa and the Middle East."[26] Ye'or's detailed analysis shows us the various ways in which this slow-motion suicide has taken place, and the interests and pathologies that facilitated this appeasement. The key instrument in this process was the establishment in 1973 of the Euro-Arab Dialogue (EAD) by the European Economic

Community, the precursor of the E.U. This group has created a vision of relations between Europe and the Muslim states of North Africa and the Middle East in which Islamic cultural superiority, hostility to Israel and America, "human, economic, and political symbiosis" between Europe and the Muslim world, and European colonial and imperial guilt are the fundamental components.[27]

The immediate factors in the creation of Eurabia were political and economic self-interest and fear, triggered by the 1973 Arab oil embargo that followed Israel's victory in the Yom Kippur war. France particularly took the lead in cultivating its ex-colonial possessions in North Africa and the Middle East to create a counterweight to postwar American power, with the added bonus of gaining access to oil, immigrant labor, and markets in the Middle East, especially for weapons. Most important, Europe would receive protection from the terrorist attacks that throughout the 1970s became a potent weapon in the new jihad against the West. The creation of the EAD was followed by numerous other organs of European-Arab rapprochement, such as the Parliamentary Association for Euro-Arab Cooperation, all funded by European taxpayers. For the Arabs, recognition and support of the Palestinian Liberation Organization and its demands, along with the demonization of Israel, were the price for easing European fears of terrorism and for opening Arab markets to European businesses. And acknowledgment of Muslim claims to cultural superiority, and of European colonial and imperial guilt, was demanded as well.

The superiority of Islamic civilization to European, and the latter's presumed cultural debt to the former, has become a staple of Eurabian propaganda. The Muslim occupation of Spain for seven centuries, the consequence of Islamic imperialistic jihad, is turned into an enlightened rule characterized by ecumenical tolerance and peaceful coexistence, the so-called "golden age" of Andalusia. As Ye'or observes, "This 'golden age' of blissful

Andalusian dhimmitude for the Christian Spanish majority and the Jews in the Middle Ages would provide a model for the social and political projects of Euro-Arab fusion in the twenty-first century."[28] The facts of the Muslim occupation of Spain, however, are very different from such fantasies. Muslim rule in Spain was characterized by Jim Crow-like laws codifying Christian and Jewish inferiority, frequent raids, the payment of oppressive tribute, and massacres like the pogrom in Granada in 1066, which killed between three thousand and four thousand Jews.[29] Moses Maimonides, the twelfth-century Jewish philosopher and physician who lived under Muslim rule, wrote after fleeing Muslim Spain for Egypt, "[T]he Arabs have persecuted us severely, and passed baneful and discriminatory legislation against us. . . . Never did a nation molest, degrade, debase, and hate us as much as they."[30] Though historically false, the myth of the Andalusian golden age legitimizes the calls to Islamize a European culture now depicted as corrupt and exhausted, neatly fusing Muslim arrogance with Western self-loathing.

Such idealizations of Islamic culture also serve as a reproach to a Western civilization seen as overly materialistic and individualistic—a critique, by the way, that reinforces the neo-Marxist criticism of capitalism as distorting human consciousness and relations to serve the soul-killing profit motive. The most egregious example of this erroneous idealization of Islam has come from England's heir to the throne, Charles, Prince of Wales. For decades he has beat the drum for the superiority of Islam to his own culture, recycling Romantic clichés about Western materialism and the "disenchantment of nature" allegedly perpetrated by science: "Islam," he announced in 1993, "can teach us today a way of understanding and living in the world which Christianity itself is poorer for having lost. At the heart of Islam is its preservation of an integral view of the Universe. Islam—like Buddhism and Hinduism—

refuses to separate man and nature, religion and science, mind and matter, and has preserved a metaphysical and unified view of ourselves and the world around us. . . . But the West gradually lost this integrated vision of the world with Copernicus and Descartes and the coming of the scientific revolution. A comprehensive philosophy of nature is no longer part of our everyday beliefs."[31] Filled with such historical errors and clichés, Charles has lobbied for Islamic instruction in public schools, alleging that Islam preserves an "integrated, spiritual view of the world in a way we have not seen fit to do in recent generations in the West," and defending his call for more Muslim teachers by saying "we need to be taught by Islamic teachers how to learn with our hearts, as well as our heads."[32] Without telling us why an admittedly needed spiritual regeneration cannot come from the Judeo-Christian tradition that created the West, Charles simply denigrates his own culture in favor of one that seeks to destroy it.

We see here one of the roots of the current E.U. problems with its Muslim immigrants, who are allowed or even encouraged to reject assimilation partly because of this acceptance of Europe's cultural inferiority and historical guilt. What is worse, this loss of faith in Western civilization on the part of Europeans is paralleled by their refusal to bear children, all the while that immigrant numbers are increasing. For those waging jihad by other means, the influx of Muslim immigrants into Europe, consistently championed by the EAD, is a demographic weapon: fecund Muslim immigrants will in time overwhelm Europeans who refuse to reproduce, exactly what is occurring today in many parts of Europe. Because of illegal immigration, "family unification" programs, and hidden polygamy—one British report in 2004 estimated that as many as four thousand Muslims avoided illegal polygamy by marrying in religious ceremonies—demographers can only guess at the numbers of immigrants and their reproduction rates.[33] This conquest through demography was explicitly articulated in 1974 by Algerian president Houari Boumédienne, who said in the U.N., "One day millions of men will leave the southern hemisphere of this planet to burst into the northern one. But not as friends. Because they will burst in to conquer, and they will conquer by populating it with their children. Victory will come to us from the wombs of our women."[34] The demography weapon is regularly brandished by contemporary jihadists: "We cannot conquer these people [Westerners] with tanks and troops," an Iranian mullah told London-based Middle-East expert Hazhir Temourian, "so we have got to overcome them by force of numbers."[35] And more recently a mullah in Norway boasted, "Just look at the development within Europe, where the number of Muslims is expanding like mosquitoes. By 2050, 30 percent of the population in Europe will be Muslim."[36]

Moreover, part of the Eurabian program is the assertion that the host countries have an obligation to adapt to these multiplying immigrants rather than the other way around. At the EAD's Hamburg Symposium in 1983, workshops recommended that host countries make every effort to learn about, understand, celebrate, and adapt to the culture of the immigrant, including offering instruction in their native languages, and presenting Arabic and Muslim culture in highly positive terms. No reciprocal efforts on the part of immigrants were recommended. Bat Ye'or summarizes the appeasing tone of this and other such symposia: "The Europeans are cautious and emphasize their respectful admiration for Islam. They pay excessive tribute to the great Islamic civilization from which the civilization of Europe has allegedly drawn inspiration. . . . They formulate platitudinous, humble excuses for colonization and Europe's anti-Arab prejudices. The Arab side's representatives, on the other hand, adopt the tone of a schoolteacher wielding the stick."[37]

This apologetic attitude towards immigrants is captured in a statement by a French priest made in the eighties, during the influx of "asylum seekers": "To help the immigrants, we must first of all respect them as they are and as they want to be according to their national identity, their cultural specificity, their spiritual and religious heritage."[38] Just this sort of self-loathing appeasement went on to characterize broader E.U. immigration policy: "The agreements between the E.C./E.U. and the Arab League," Ye'or writes, "facilitated the exportation of the immigrants' culture to the host countries as an inalienable right of the immigrants. It has created an obstacle to their integration—all the more so as the bonds with the countries of emigration were encouraged and supported to the utmost by cultural, political, and economic agreements between European and Arab governments."[39]

This self-abasing posture and acknowledgement of Muslim superiority has traditionally characterized the *dhimmi* whose fate is to be subordinated to Islam. As for the *jizya*, the poll tax the *dhimmi* must pay to their Muslim overlords, the billions in social-welfare transfers to immigrants, not to mention the billions more sent by the E.U. to Middle Eastern regimes and terrorist organizations such as the Palestinian Liberation Organization and its offspring, the Palestinian Authority—about $750 million from the E.U. and the U.N. in 2006 alone—are simply the tribute due to the spiritual superior from the humiliated spiritual inferior. According to Kheir Sajer, a Norwegian Muslim critical of Islam, some European Muslim leaders explicitly encourage taking advantage of, or even cheating, the host countries' social welfare generosity, rationalizing such behavior as exacting the *jizya* justified by Islamic law.[40]

If economic and political self-interest was the dynamic for creating Eurabia, the cultural toxins that followed the loss of faith and that have been poisoning Europe for the last two centuries

facilitated the demonization of the Western way and the idealization of Islam. Having accepted its guilt for all the world's ills,
and lacking its traditional spiritual resources, the West cannot
resist the fanatic aggression of those who are supremely confident
in the rightness of their faith and its sanction by the divine.

Key to this failure of Western nerve that makes Eurabia possible is the doctrine of multiculturalism that permeates the thinking of Western elites. The essence of multiculturalism is not, as is
often claimed, the call to recognize and respect the value and contributions of other cultures, something the West has been doing
for ages. Indeed, a fascination with alien peoples and their ways
has been a hallmark of the West going back to the ancient Greeks.
In Herodotus's *History*, the entire second book is devoted to
Egypt, whose civilization is presented in an admiring light. Western culture has profited from this curiosity and openness to other
cultures, whose ideas Westerners have cheerfully borrowed or
stolen. Linked to this openness to the cultural "other" is another
invention peculiar to the Greeks and then the West: critical consciousness, the willingness to look at one's own ways and hold
them up to scrutiny and even rejection. Such openness to the foreigner and self-criticism are unusual in most human societies,
which accept their own ways uncritically and view the foreigner
with distrust, intolerance, or contempt.

Yet this openness to the cultural "other" and willingness to
criticize one's own ways have degenerated into a naïve idealization of the non-Westerner and a corresponding hatred of the
West, both of which make up the ideological core of multiculturalism. Using idealized primitive cultures to criticize one's own
is as old as civilization itself. All civilizations have had some version of the "noble savage," that creature who lives a simple life in
harmony with nature, without the government, law, private property, wealth, and technology that presumably make the civilized

so miserable. The Sumerians had Enkidu, the Greeks the Scythians, and the Romans the Germanic tribes, whose simple, hardy lives reproached the decadence of imperial Rome. These imagined peoples—I say imagined since the actual lives of most primitive peoples have been filled with hardship, violence, oppression, malnutrition, and pain—are useful sticks for beating one's own corrupt and complicated civilization even as one has no intention of leaving it for the "celestial and majestic simplicity of man before corruption by society," as Jean-Jacques Rousseau put it.[41]

This ancient myth became more attractive when Europe began to industrialize and urbanize in the eighteenth century. The advent of smoke-belching factories, crowded slums, huge cities shrouded in coal smoke, railroads, new forms of mass communication, and the social disruptions that followed gave new force to these old complaints about civilization. At the same time, the primitive, exotic peoples Europeans had been encountering since the discovery of the Americas seemed to embody a simpler, more humane existence that the West had abandoned in its pursuit of power and profit. American Indians, South Sea Islanders, Africans, Arabs—these were the new "noble savages" described by seventeenth-century English poet John Dryden, the "guiltless men, that danced away their time/Fresh as their groves and happy as their climes," for they all seemed to live lives more natural and meaningful, more truly human and fulfilling than the harried, polluted, complex, noisy existence of Western man, penned in his dirty cities and enslaved to money, science, and technology.[42]

This use of "noble savages" to reproach a decadent European civilization became a staple of Romanticism. As early as 1828, German poet Johann Wolfgang von Goethe expressed this Romantic trope when he wrote, "We other Europeans are ailing. Our styles of life are far from the healthy state of nature, and our social relations lack charity and benevolence." Linked to this dissatisfaction with one's own culture is an idealization of superior primitive cultures: "I often wish," Goethe continued, "I were one of these so-called savages born in the islands of the South Seas, so that at least once I could savor human existence in its purity, without some artificial aftertaste."[43] These Romantic complaints have dominated the art and literature of the West for the last two centuries. They formed as well the core assumptions of the new "science" of anthropology, which stopped "indulging the vanity of Europeans," French social critic Alain Finkielkraut notes, "and began nurturing their guilty conscience instead," reducing Westerners to just one more primitive tribe, no better—and frequently much worse—than any other.[44] Thus, what were traditionally understood as myths or literary motifs have slowly been transformed by pseudo-sciences like anthropology into facts.

In a similar fashion, these age-old mythic longings and literary themes were transmuted by later varieties of Marxism into presumably factual descriptions of historical development, and thus acquired a patina of scientific authority and political morality. Marx agreed with the Romantics about the destructive effects of industrial capitalism, which in his analysis created "alienation" and social injustice by replacing the humane, organic relations between people with the "cash nexus," as Thomas Carlyle put it, the alienating, dehumanizing power of the contract, private property, wage labor, and the profit motive. Of course, Marx thought that technical progress at the service of history's grand design would eventually restore that lost organic unity, unlike the techno-phobic Romantics, who looked to recover an imagined simpler past.[45] Yet the Romantic discontent with the modern West and its defining structures, capitalism and liberal democracy, and the elitist disdain of consumerism and mass culture, both found a seemingly scientific validation and a political program in socialism and Marxism.

Idealizations of the non-West also found reinforcement in later Marxist analyses of imperialism and colonialism. Before Marx himself died, the failure of his theory of historical development was obvious. The working class did not become more miserable, the middle class did not disappear, class war did not break out, the communist revolution did not take place in advanced industrial societies, the rate of profit did not diminish, nor did market economies hinder technological progress.[46] Precisely the opposite of all these predictions took place. One solution to this failure was to turn to European colonies and imperialism to find the coming revolution that had failed to materialize in Europe.

Marx himself had nothing but contempt for the more primitive and less technologically advanced non-European countries. After the 1846 war between Mexico and the U.S., Marx approved of California's being snatched "from the lazy Mexicans, who did not know what to do with it."[47] But in the later theorizing of Rudolf Hilferding, Nikolai Bukharin, and Vladimir Lenin, the manifestations of the contradictions of capitalism missing in Europe were displaced onto the Third World, and imperialism became the means by which capitalism avoided or postponed all the destructive consequences predicted by Marx. Now revolution was more likely to break out "where the concentration of contradictions was greatest, i.e. on the fringe of the capitalist world, in backward, colonial, or semi-colonial countries."[48] Anti-colonial revolutions and independence movements in the Third World were now to be supported and fomented because they served the inevitable progress of the global communist revolution. As Jean-Paul Sartre put it, in his introduction to Frantz Fanon's 1963 anti-colonial screed *The Wretched of the Earth*, "Natives of all the underdeveloped countries unite!"[49] Because of this idealization of the Third World as history's instrument for transforming the wicked West, resistance to immigration, demands that immigrants assimilate to their new homes, and expressions of national pride have all become "fascist," tainted with Nazi racism and the Holocaust.

Indeed, as Paul Gottfried argues, this congeries of debased Marxist attitudes to the Third World "other" constitutes a new political religion, one that "emphasizes the radical polarization between the multicultural Good and the xenophobic Evil and is willing to apply force to suppress those considered wicked. Like older political religions, Post-Marxism also claims to be pointing the way toward a future in which the remnants of the adversary (still vestigially bourgeois) society are swept aside." Understanding post-Marxist multiculturalism as a "would-be successor to a traditional belief system, one parasitic on Judeo-Christian symbols but equipped with its own transformational myths and end-of-history vision," explains the multicultural left's resistance to empirical facts about the unique goods of Western civilization and the threat posed to them by a resurgent Islam.[50]

Naïve idealizations of the Third World thus have become for "leftists" the basis for pursuing the liberation of the oppressed and the transformation of a hated bourgeois capitalist society, all the while that such "anti-imperialism" ignored the very brutal imperialist ambitions of the Soviet Union, and now shrugs off the current expansionist aggression of the jihadists. This mixture of noble-savage idealism, Romantic discontent with modernity, Marxist-Leninist theorizing, and post-Marxist multiculturalism has created Third Worldism, the doctrine that "every Westerner is presumed guilty until proven innocent," as French social critic Pascal Bruckner puts it in his brilliant analysis *The Tears of the White Man*. "We Europeans have been raised to detest ourselves, certain that, within our world, there is a certain essential evil that must be relentlessly atoned for. This evil is known by two terms— colonialism and imperialism."[51] This self-hatred becomes positively suicidal among many Westerners who, convinced of their guilt, do not have the cultural resources for defending their way of life against those who would destroy it. They seem to have accepted, as Sartre matter-of-factly put it, that "Europe is done for."[52] And these days the successor of Europe is Eurabia.

One can see how these attitudes vitiate the assimilation of immigrants into European cultures. Since their home cultures are superior to the guilty decadent West that has exploited and victimized them, they are encouraged to cling to the old ways, even though the immigrants themselves have voted with their feet against their countries of origin, and even though those cultures legitimize practices that violate Western ideals of freedom and individual rights. "For fear of doing violence to individual immigrants," Finkielkraut writes, "we confuse these new arrivals with the uniforms fashioned for them by history. To let them live as they like, we refuse to protect them from the misdeeds or eventual abuses they might experience at the hands of their own traditions."[53] This indifference has certainly been the experience of many Muslim immigrants, particularly women, who are subjected to beatings, honor killings, forced marriages, genital mutilation, and other practices validated by Islamic or tribal culture.

Because of multiculturalism, then, Muslim immigrants have been allowed to perpetuate their cultures no matter how alien to the values of Western civilization even as the European nations make it difficult for those who do wish to assimilate. Immigrant communities are allowed to create their own standards of behavior, educational curricula, social mores, and public practices, indulgences not allowed native-born citizens of the host countries. In Sweden, for example, the legal age of marriage is eighteen, but for immigrants there is no minimum age. A German who wishes to marry someone not from an E.U. member state must answer an intrusive list of questions to prove the marriage's legitimacy, a requirement not demanded of Germans with Turkish or Pakistani backgrounds, on the assumption that their marriages are arranged.[54] French public swimming pools are segregated by sex to appease Muslim sensibilities, and some British retailers have stopped selling mugs that depict A. A. Milne's Piglet because Muslims find pigs offensive. Burger King's chocolate ice cream swirls were banished because they reminded some Muslims of Arabic writing. After the murder of Dutch filmmaker Theo van Gogh, Dutch schoolchildren were not allowed to wear Dutch flags on their backpacks lest Muslims find them provocative.[55]

The appeasement of Muslim separatism is most evident in the proliferation of schools teaching immigrant children how to be Muslims rather than citizens of their home countries. In Germany, religious instruction provided by the Islamic Federation of Berlin, linked to extremist Islamic groups, can now be found in twenty-eight Berlin schools. Lower Saxony offers Islamic classes in eight elementary schools, a program overseen by local Islamic organizations. Such schools are getting started in Bavaria as well. England has 110 Islamic schools.[56] In February 2007, the Muslim Council of Britain issued a set of guidelines for public schools that, if followed, would lead to a de facto institution of Islamic *sharia* law in British schools.[57] As for the curriculum, at a Saudi-funded school in Bonn, an undercover German journalist filmed racist and anti-Western lessons, and a similar school in London was exposed using textbooks slandering Jews and Christians.[58]

These indulgent double standards—abetted by a sense of entitlement to redress for presumed European historical crimes—make more difficult the identification of immigrants with their host countries rather than with the larger Muslim community. Numerous public opinion polls have documented this alienation among many Muslim immigrants, particularly after the terrorist attacks in New York, London, and Madrid. In England, ten surveys, eight completed after the July 2005 terrorist bombings, revealed that a majority of British Muslims see a conflict between their Muslim and British identities, significantly more of them identifying with their religion than with England. Forty percent approve of *sharia*, Islamic religious law, being applied in Muslim areas, and 36 percent believe that British values threaten the Muslim way of life.[59] This conflict between Islamic faith and national identity is found throughout Europe. Jytte Klausen's surveys on Muslim attitudes to "mainstreaming" Islam found that 61 percent are opposed. Of that group, 28 percent are what Klausen calls "neo-orthodox," those "who think that Western norms are incompatible with the exercise of Islam and oppose the integration of Islamic institutions to existing European frameworks for the exercise of religion."[60]

The new thought-crime of "Islamophobia," a variation of the "racist" charge used by multiculturalists to forestall criticism or even statements of patent facts, illustrates how far the European establishment has gone in abandoning its own values, such as free speech and a respect for truth, in order to appease a vocal minority. This new "crime," frequently equated by Islamic radicals with the Holocaust, is now in widespread use in order to make Europeans guilty for whatever dysfunctions exist among Muslim immigrants. It was launched in 1997 by a British think tank, the Runnymede Trust, in a report trying to explain the problems of Muslims. True to the therapeutic delusions and self-loathing of the European establishment, the authors fingered the "anti-Islamic bias" that distorted public discussions of Islam and Muslims: "This bias," Jytte Klausen summarizes the report, "fostered discrimination in employment and schooling, hate crimes, mischaracterization in the media and in everyday life, and a range of other problems experienced by Muslims."[61] In 2004, this analysis was repeated by the Commission on British Muslims and Islamophobia, which concluded that England was "institutionally Islamophobic."[62] The problem is, those supposedly false prejudices about Islam, such as its treatment of women and its intolerance of other faiths, are in fact true for significant numbers of Muslims. Even Klausen, whose book is sympathetic to Muslim immigrants, faults such analyses for "fail[ing] to acknowledge the anti-liberal strains within some versions of Islam, the anti-Western rhetoric of an uncomfortably large number of Muslim groups and radical clerics, and the real support offered to terrorism by a tiny but highly publicized and perhaps truly dangerous minority."[63]

Europe thus harbors within its nations a significant number of people who are alienated from Western civilization and believe it to be inimical to their faith. And these attitudes are reinforced by the institutionalized self-loathing on the part of European elites, who are eager to don the colonialist and imperialist hair shirt and appease those who demand concessions, no matter how incompatible with the core values of Western civilization. Unsurprisingly, the Eurabian neurosis has led to the appeasement of terrorist and terrorist sympathizers who have made crystal-clear their hatred of the West and their willingness to use violence against it.

SERIAL MUNICHS

The train bombings in Madrid on March 11, 2004, and the subway and bus bombings in London on July 7, 2005, were simply the grisly, spectacular manifestations of the long-festering problems resulting from Europe's cultural failure of nerve and appeasement of those who want to destroy the West. As much as the attacks themselves, the reactions to them on the part of many European politicians and intellectuals were themselves revealing. On the very day that fifty-two Londoners were killed, a police official asserted for the television cameras, "Islam and terrorists are two words that do not go together." This statement was consistent with official police policy never to use the phrase "Islamic terrorism." This policy of ignoring the very clear beliefs expressed by terrorists to justify their murders is reflected as well in police commissioner Sir Ian Blair's astonishing claim that "There is nothing wrong with being an Islamic fundamentalist."[64] Apparently, blowing up commuters is "nothing." London's leftist mayor, Ken Livingstone, predictably put the blame on the West for "eighty years of Western intervention into predominantly Arab lands because of the Western need for oil."[65] Prime Minister Tony Blair seemed to understand the nature of the threat. He set up a committee to correct the "evil ideology" presumably warping young Muslim minds, but then the government put on the committee members like lawyer Ahmad Thomson, who believes a cabal of Jews and Freemasons controls the governments of Europe and America, and Inayat Bunglawala. This "moderate" has called Osama bin Laden a "freedom fighter," refuses without equivocation to condemn Palestinian terrorism, and alleges that the British media are "Zionist-controlled."[66]

The reaction in Spain to the terrorist murder of one hundred ninety-one Spaniards was even more redolent of groveling dhimmitude. Eleven and a half million people, nearly one-third of the population, took to the streets in mass demonstrations—mostly to protest against conservative Spanish president José María Aznar, whose support for the U.S. invasion of Iraq was blamed for the attacks. Three days after the bombs went off, Spain put into power the Socialist candidate, José Luis Rodriguez Zapatero, who promised to move Spain away from the U.S. and closer to Europe, which in practical terms meant removing Spanish troops from Iraq. The terrorists had timed their attacks before the election precisely to intimidate the Spaniards withdrawing from Iraq. An Al Qaeda document made public after the bombing speculated correctly that Spain "cannot suffer more than two to three strikes before pulling out [from Iraq] under pressure from its own peo-ple."[67] Al Qaeda's only mistake was thinking it would take more than one "strike." The same Spanish people whose ancestors had fought for seven centuries to drive the imperialist Muslims from Spain had now justified their status as *dhimmi*, spiritual inferiors whose deserved fate is to be subordinated to Islam.

Yet these craven responses to terrorist murder are consistent with the indulgence with which many European governments have long treated numerous radical Muslims. In 2003, the Dutch government allowed the Arab European League to open a branch in the Netherlands. The league was founded in Belgium by Dyab Abou Jahjah, who once belonged to the terrorist organization Hezbollah. Jahjah called the terrorist attacks of September 11 "sweet revenge," and later expressed admiration for the Madrid bombers. His political goal is to implement *sharia*, Islamic law, throughout Europe. Leaders of the Netherlands Arab European League have called for the destruction of Israel and the stoning of homosexuals, and approved of Moroccan youths chanting "Gas all the Jews" in the streets of Amsterdam.

Yet such blindness is not a problem just for the Dutch. As Claire Berlinski writes, "Throughout Europe, funded by foreign money, thousands of mosques import a belligerent strain of Islam that rejects assimilation and embraces jihad." An imam in Stras-bourg has founded a party whose platform demonizes Jews and denies the Holocaust, and the imam of Hamburg's al-Quds mosque —which was attended by 9/11 terrorist Mohamed Atta—preached before 9/11 that "the Jews and crusaders must have their throats slit."[68] In Italy, a "leader" of the Piedmont Islamic community praises jihad as "right and justified," and an imam in Bologna blamed 9/11 on the Americans and Israelis and proclaimed Osama bin Laden's innocence—this a few days after a pamphlet praising terrorism was distributed in Bologna's mosque.[69] Mullah Krekar,

who founded the Kurdish terrorist organization Ansar al-Islam
and called 9/11 a "gift from Allah," received in the late nineties
$35,000 from the Norwegian government for an organization he
created called Islamic Vision, before he went to Iraq to organize
terrorist attacks. The government of Jordan charged him with
plotting attacks against Israelis and Americans, yet Norway let
him walk away. Despite subsequent calls for violence, for which he
was indicted, all charges against him eventually were dropped,
and he received 45,000 euros from a Dutch court in compensation for his imprisonment.[70]

The French are responsible for one of the most outrageous acts
of terrorist appeasement. During the Seventies and Eighties France's
sanctuary doctrine allowed terrorists to live in France as long as
they didn't attack French interests. After arresting Daoud Oudeh,
founder of the Black September group responsible for massacring
Israeli athletes at the 1972 Olympics, France ignored extradition
requests from Israel and Germany and sent him instead to Alge-
ria.[71] And let's not forget that in the seventies France sheltered
the Ayatollah Khomeini, who returned to Iran to create a regime
that is one of the world's foremost supporters of jihadist terror.

England, however, has taken the lead in repeatedly sheltering
and subsidizing radical Muslims who openly declare their hatred
of the West and the legitimacy of violence. Abu Qatada, a veteran
of the jihad in Afghanistan who has been called "Osama bin
Laden's European ambassador," turned up in London, where he
published a newspaper for an Algerian terrorist organization and
established connections to terrorist cells in Germany, France and
Italy. Omar Bakri Mohammed, founder of the Islamist Hizb ut-
Tahrir, publicly and with impunity called for the assassination of
British prime minister John Major; his goal preached to his fol-
lowers is "flying the Islamic flag over Downing Street." Worse yet,
Bakri was receiving 300 pounds a week in welfare benefits up to

the time he left the country after the July 2005 terrorist attacks. As Melanie Phillips summarizes in her invaluable study, "Terrorists wanted in other countries were given safe haven in the United Kingdom and left free to foment hatred against the West. Extremist groups such as Hizb ut-Tahrir remained legal. . . . Radicals such as Abu Qatada, Omar Bakri Mohammed, Abu Hamza, and Mohammed al-Massari were allowed to preach incitement to violence, raise money, and recruit members for the jihad. An astonishing procession of U.K.-based terrorists turned out to have been responsible for attacks upon America, Israel, and many other countries."[72]

Europe's cultural sickness, however, is most evident in the flaccid response to radical Muslim assaults on core Western values such as free speech. The death sentence imposed in 1989 by Iran's Ayatollah Khomeini on Indian novelist Salman Rushdie was merely the first in a series of violent reactions to Western expressions of free thought. Rushdie had to go into hiding for many years, and in England Muslims burned his books in the streets and publicly called for his murder. More significant, however, was the response of the British political establishment, ranging from the tepid statement that such threats were "totally unacceptable," to historian Lord Dacre's comment that he "would not shed a tear if some British Muslims, deploring Mr. Rushdie's manners, were to waylay him in a dark street and seek to improve them." As Melanie Phillips notes, this episode encapsulated European appeasement of those scorning the most cherished values of the West.[73]

Since 9/11, such episodes have proliferated. One of the most gruesomely spectacular was the murder of Dutch filmmaker Theo van Gogh, a relative of the great painter. Van Gogh's crime was to make an eleven-minute-long film, with Somalian immigrant and critic of Islam Ayaan Hirsi Ali, about the brutal subjection of women under Islamic custom and religious law. Two months after *Submission* aired in August 2004, van Gogh was shot and stabbed to death on an Amsterdam street, his throat cut with a butcher's knife, and a five-page letter stuck to his chest. The letter called for the murder of Hirsi Ali and the destruction of Europe and America. Hirsi Ali, a member of parliament, had to live under police protection until she left for the United States, where she now resides. Another member of parliament, Geert Wilders, likewise had to live in seclusion under police protection because he called for closing down radical mosques.[74]

Van Gogh's murderer, Mohammed Bouyeri, like the London bombers was a recipient of welfare largess who associated with a Syrian radical named Abou Khaled. Khaled is another example of Europe's suicidally undiscriminating immigration policies. He preached that Muslims who deviated from Islamic laws were infidels who should be killed, and that democracy was incompatible with Islam. The group Bouyeri belonged to that met with Khaled included two brothers who plotted to blow up the houses of parliament, and possibly had links with other European jihadist organizations. The group's favorite pastime was watching DVDs that depicted terrorists cutting the throats of infidels. Tutored by Khaled, Bouyeri believed that "to withdraw from the infidels means hating them, being their enemy, being revolted by them, loathing them, and fighting them." Several members of the group were picked up by the Dutch authorities, but were quickly released.[75]

More than Bouyeri's existence, the reaction of Dutch society to the murder testifies to how deeply the appeasing mentality of the *dhimmi* has lodged in the European psyche. At his trial, Bouyeri clearly articulated the Islamic motivation for the murder of van Gogh: "So the story that I felt insulted as a Moroccan, or because he called me a goat fucker, that is all nonsense. I acted out of faith. And I made it clear that if it had been my own father, or my little brother, I would have done the same thing." He went on to tell the court that his religious obligations included cutting off the heads of "all those who insult Allah and his prophet," and that living in a country with free speech was contrary to Islamic law. He finished by saying that if he were freed, he would do exactly the same thing.[76]

These clearly expressed religious motives, however, consistent with centuries of Islamic theology, jurisprudence, and practice, nonetheless were never accepted at face value. Instead, they were reduced to expressions of some psychological trauma connected to inequitable social and economic conditions, as when Bouyeri's former history teacher blamed a lack of jobs for young immigrants' attraction to radical Islam.[77] In other words, the pseudo-religion of a secularized Europe that no longer can take faith seriously trumped the very real religious motive of the murderer. This reduction of all behavior to environmental determinism fed as well many Europeans' refusal to judge evil and identify clearly its causes. When after van Gogh's murder, deputy prime minister Gerrit Zalm said that the Netherlands was at war with Islamic extremism, a Green leader huffed, "We fall too easily into an 'us' and 'them' antithesis with the word 'war.'" Similarly, a socialist politician opined, "If rationality is pushed aside, hate could lodge itself in the heads of extremists."[78] Such moral relativism demonstrates to the jihadists that the West is ripe for destruction.

Across Europe, the same tepid or self-loathing responses to a brutal attack on cherished Western artistic and political values were evident. There were maudlin appeals to "tolerance" and "respect," without any awareness that these very values were rejected by van Gogh's killer and many other Muslims, who see no reason to tolerate or respect those who do not share their beliefs. The left-wing *Guardian* in England suggested that van Gogh had it coming because of his "magnificent disregard for the feelings [he] might be offending." One journalist characterized criticism of Islam as "bashing," and advised his countrymen to

accept the "risk of Islamic fundamentalist violence" just as smok-
ers accept the risk of cancer. As for the so-called moderate Dutch
Muslims presumably offended by Bouyeri's "hijacking" of their
faith, hardly any of them showed up for a rally in protest of terrorist violence, while tens of thousands of Muslims regularly
assemble across Europe to march against America and Israel, not
to mention the hundreds of thousands who celebrated in jubila-
tion after 9/11.[79] The refusal to clearly identify the enemy who
has declared war on you, the recourse to an environmental determinism that ignores the enemy's spiritually validated choices and
motives, and the failure to judge evil all bespeak the therapeutic
superstitions that have replaced Christianity in the European
worldview.

Such episodes of appeasement in the face of Islamic aggression
are each a little Munich, a failure of nerve as dangerous as England's
capitulation to Hitler's murderous ambitions—as Islamic scholar
Bernard Lewis has put it, "We seem to be in the mode of Cham-
berlain and Munich rather than of Churchill."[80] After 9/11, Italian journalist Oriana Fallaci published *The Rage and the Pride*, her
best-selling, impassioned defense of Western civilization and its
unique goods, which earned her death threats from Muslims all over
the world. Europe's ruling elite responded to this defense of all that
Europe claims to hold dear, such as free speech and free thought,
by trying to prosecute her as a criminal. The Berne Federal Office
of Justice, egged on by groups like the Islamic Center of Berne, in
November 2002 unsuccessfully asked the Italian government to
extradite Fallaci so she could be prosecuted under Switzerland's
Article 261B, an anti-racism statute elastic enough to cover any criticism of Islam whatsoever. The indictment accused her of "racist
behaviour" and ideas which "endanger public peace and generate
hate among those who believe in the clash of civilizations"—in
other words, Fallaci was indicted for an idea.[81] She was also sued in

French court over the same book, a suit she won. Then in May 2005, an Italian judge charged her with writing in *The Force of Reason*, her follow-up book published in 2004, passages that are "without doubt offensive to Islam and to those who practice that religious faith."[82] Given that Fallaci could have been arrested anywhere in Europe under the E.U.'s European arrest warrant, she moved to New York, where she died of cancer while awaiting trial.

The important Western idea of the free press likewise came under assault by jihadists, who in February 2006 ignited a worldwide violent protest by Muslims over a Dutch newspaper's reprint of innocuous cartoons depicting Muhammad. While some Europeans rushed to defend the freedom of the press, and many newspapers reprinted the cartoons in solidarity, other reactions evinced the self-loathing appeasement of a civilization that no longer believes in its own values. When the Organization of the Islamic Conference and the Arab League demanded a resolution banning "contempt for religious beliefs," the U.N. High Commissioner for Human Rights said, "I find alarming any behaviors that disregard the beliefs of others," and started an investigation into "racism" and "disrespect for belief," apparently unconcerned with the assault on the Western belief in free speech and a free press.[83] Similarly blind to the assault on Western values, the E.U.'s justice minister announced the creation of a "media code" to encourage "prudence," which is just another way of endorsing censorship.[84] In Italy, a politician who distributed T-shirts printed with the cartoons was forced to resign after Libyans stormed the Italian consulate in Benghazi. He hastened to assure the world that "it was never my intention to offend the Muslim religion."[85] A Danish dairy, chafing over business lost because of a boycott in the Middle East, said, "We understand and respect your [Muslims'] reaction" to this "irresponsible and regrettable incident."[86] Across Europe, web sites were shut down and journalists were charged as

European governments pressured newspapers not to reprint the cartoons. As *Sunday Times* columnist Jasper Gerard wrote, "Islam is protected by an invisible blasphemy law. It is called fear."[87]

Such groveling appeasement of assaults on the core values of Western civilization fits the profile of the *dhimmi* as documented by Bat Ye'or. To many Muslims, the Europeans' capitulation to threats and violence bespeaks the spiritual poverty of a people for whom the highest good is physical comfort and pleasure, and nothing exists that is worth fighting and dying for. The indifference of Europe to violence against Christians and Jews in Middle Eastern countries-such as the *jihadist* murder in 2001 of seventeen Christians in Pakistan, or the desecration of Christian churches —while Europeans fret over and apologize for the most trivial "insults" to Islam, also confirms the decadence of the West and the superiority of Islam. What else are they to think, when a huge mosque is being built in Rome, while not a single church or synagogue exists in Saudi Arabia? Likewise, the European demonization of Israel, a Western democracy, reinforces the traditional Muslim disdain for Jews, and has provided cover for a resurgence of one of Europe's most pernicious cultural diseases, anti-Semitism.

HATING JEWS

A U.S. State Department Survey has reported that in Europe "beginning in 2000, verbal attacks directed against Jews increased while incidents of vandalism (e.g. graffiti, fire bombings of Jewish schools, desecration of synagogues and cemeteries) surged. Physical assaults, including beatings, stabbings, and other violence against Jews in Europe, increased markedly, in a number of cases resulting in serious injury and even death." Though significant numbers of these attacks originate with neo-Nazi and far-right groups, "disadvantaged and disaffected Muslim youths increasingly were responsible for most of the other incidents."[88]

One of the most gruesome crimes was the murder of Ilan Halimi, a 23-year-old Jewish man from Baneux, France. In February 2006, Halimi was kidnapped, tortured for three weeks, burned with acid, stabbed, and then left to die in the woods. During his ordeal, the kidnappers told Halimi's family to get the money from a synagogue, and later told a rabbi, "We have a Jew." Some of the suspects when questioned admitted they targeted Halimi because Jews are rich. According to some reports, they tortured him because he was Jewish. Most of the gang who murdered Halimi were Muslims, and most of the victims targeted in other attempted kidnappings were Jewish. A search of one gang member's home turned up Islamist literature. Numerous people near the mostly French-Arab housing project where Halimi was confined knew he was there, yet no one alerted the police.[89] This murder recalled an earlier one from 2003, when a French-Algerian murdered a Jewish disk jockey, slitting his throat and gouging out his eyes. He told his mother, "I killed my Jew; I will go to paradise."[90]

Despite the steady increase of anti-Semitic attacks tied to Muslim immigrants, most European politicians refuse to identify Islam as a factor in these crimes. A report commissioned by the E.U. in November 2003 that identified "radical Islamists or young Muslims, mostly of Arab descent" as perpetrators of anti-Semitic attacks was suppressed, then followed up six months later by another that denied any link at all to Muslims.[91] Even when Muslims are acknowledged to be behind attacks, either economic and social deprivation are offered as excuses, or the attacks are usually explained as "a direct outcome of the festering crisis in the Middle East," as Tony Judt rationalizes them.[92] Leftist politicians continually put the blame on Israel and its policies, usually recycling the old myths of traditional Islamic "tolerance" toward Jews. Typical is the statement by French foreign minister Hubert Védrine, who in 2002 said, "One shouldn't necessarily be surprised that young French people from immigrant families feel compassion for the Palestinians and get agitated when they see what is happening."[93]

This singling out of Israel as a rogue state whose uniquely oppressive policies cause social disruption among Europe's Muslim immigrants is false to the historical evidence. As Walter Laqueur points out, since Israel's creation in 1948, millions of people have died "as the result of civil wars, repression, racial and social persecution, and tribal conflicts. . . . National and religious minority groups have been systematically persecuted, abused, raped, burned, shot, gassed, and their property demolished, from Indonesia, Pakistan, and Bangladesh, to Central Asia and beyond." Yet all this oppression and violence—often perpetrated by Muslims against fellow Muslims—have not generated a fraction of the hatred directed against Israel for trying to survive the attacks of those who have sworn its destruction. By some estimates, twenty-five million people have been killed in internal conflicts since World War II—only eight thousand in the Israeli-Arab conflict: "But Israel has been more often condemned by the United Nations and other international organizations than all other nations taken together."[94] Indeed, the U.N.'s newly fashioned Human Rights Council, created to replace the ineffective and corrupt Human Rights Commission, has issued eight condemnations since it started meeting, every single one against Israel, while gross human-rights violators like Muslim Sudan are ignored.[95]

This fixation on Israel, then, cannot be adequately explained as a reaction to Israel's behavior, or to the supposed racist ideology of Zionism. It is more likely that hatred of Israel and Zionism have become the new mask of anti-Semitism, one that avoids the opprobrium of the Holocaust and Nazism. For Muslims particularly, disdain or hatred of Jews predates the creation of Israel, and is justified by the fourteen-century-long tradition of Islamic jurisprudence and theology. In the Koran, Jews are "laden with God's anger": they are destined forever to suffer "abasement and poverty," and some of them will be turned into "apes and swine" because they rejected Muhammad's revelation. This hatred of Jews is confirmed in the centuries-long tradition of Islamic commentary on the Koran and the *hadith* or "sayings" of Muhammad. Given this traditional authority, Koranic slurs such as "apes and swine" occur repeatedly in the sermons and writings of modern jihadists and mainstream Islamic scholars. Moreover, the use of this traditional invective is regularly linked to the justification of violence against Jews, as when Sudanese dictator Omar al-Bashir called for jihad against the Jews in 2002: "Let us prepare ourselves for the decisive battle against the Jews, those apes, pigs, and worshippers of calves."[96]

This pre-existing contempt for Jews as conquered *dhimmi* who rejected Muhammad's revelation explains the attraction of fascist anti-Semitism for the Islamic Middle East. Before World War II, Arab nationalists admired German and Italian fascism, finding congenial its authoritarianism, centralization, and anti-Semitism. In the Middle East during the thirties and forties, rumors circulated that Mussolini was a secret Egyptian Muslim named Musa Nili (Moses of the Nile), and that Hitler had secretly converted to Islam.[97]

During World War II, many Middle Eastern Muslim regimes openly and secretly collaborated with the Nazis—nearly a million Muslims fought on the side of the Germans. In Egypt, proto-fascist "Green Shirts," including Anwar Sadat, schemed to help Erwin Rommel's Afrika Korps in its drive to Egypt. After the war, when rumors circulated that Hitler was still alive in Brazil, Sadat published a fawning letter of admiration to the Führer. The most notorious example of Islamic collaboration with the Nazis is the Grand Mufti of Jerusalem, Haj Amin al-Husseini, who lived in Germany until the end of the war, and then with the collusion of

Charles de Gaulle escaped prosecution for war crimes and ended up in Egypt. Al-Husseini was a rabid anti-Semite who incited three prewar massacres of Jews in Palestine. In Germany he became intimate with Hitler, and the Mufti's opposition to Jewish immigration to Palestine helped to foreclose expulsion of the Jews as a solution to the Nazi "Jewish Question."[98]

After the war, many Nazi officials and German army officers were warmly welcomed in the Middle East, where they served as military advisors and propagandists and aided guerillas fighting in North Africa. Famed Nazi commando Otto Skorzeny trained thousands of Egyptians, including Yasir Arafat, in guerilla warfare. He also organized terrorist attacks on Israel in the early fifties, and helped form the Arab Foreign Legion, which included four hundred Nazi veterans. A former assistant of Nazi propaganda chief Josef Goebbels, Johann von Leers, wrote propaganda for Egyptian president Gamal Abdel Nasser. He explained his conversion to Islam in terms that highlight the common ground between Islamic radicalism and fascism: "The Islamic bloc is today the only spiritual power in the world fighting for a real religion and human values and freedom. . . . To hell with Christianity, for in Christianity's name Germany has been sold to our oppressors!" More recently, European neo-Nazi and neo-fascist organizations have supported Islamic terrorists in various ways, from providing financial support to outright collaboration in terrorist attacks and military operations. The neo-Nazi Wehrsportgruppe-Hoffmann trained with the Palestinian Liberation Organization and fought with the Palestinians during "Black September" in 1970, the brief war between the Palestinians and the Jordanians.[99]

Particularly significant for contemporary jihadists is the work of Sayyid Qutb, the most important theoretician for modern jihad. Qutb lived in America for two years then returned to Egypt, where he was active in the Muslim Brotherhood. In his work, particularly "Our Struggle with the Jews" from the early 1950s, all the troubles of the Muslim world are attributed to "the same Jewish machinations and double-dealing which discomfited the early Muslims." He goes on to demonize the Jews for "behaving in the most disgustingly aggressive manner and sinning in the ugliest way. Everywhere the Jews have been they have committed unprecedented abominations." Qutb's solution is for Muslims to "let Allah bring down upon the Jews people who will mete out to them the worst kind of punishment." The Ayatollah Khomeini, architect of the 1979 Islamic revolution in Iran, was a disciple of Qutb. Khomeini likewise vilified the Jews, "who distorted the reputation of Islam by assaulting it and slandering it," and he called the Jews a "cancerous tumor." Similarly, the current leader of Hezbollah, Hassan Nasrallah, has called the Jews "a cancer which is liable to spread again at any moment."[100]

Today, these kinds of anti-Semitic slanders can be found throughout the Muslim world, from which, via satellite television and the Internet, they reach European Muslims. Whereas in Europe or America such Nazi-style invective is relegated to fringe minorities, in the Middle East, state-run presses, government officials, and university professors freely indulge in anti-Semitic stereotypes. Fatma Abdallah Mahmoud, a columnist for Egypt's most influential daily newspaper, the government-subsidized *Al-Akhbar*, has written that Jews are "accursed," a "catastrophe for the human race," the "plague of the generation and the bacterium of all time. Their history always was and always will be stained with treachery, falseness, and lying." A leading Saudi newspaper, *Al-Riyadh*, prints stories resurrecting the old "blood libel" that Jews use human blood to make matzo for Yom Kippur. The Palestinian daily *Al-Hayat al-Jadida* traffics in the Jew-as-Shylock slander: "They are well known for their intense love of money and its accumulaztion." And, of course, the canard of a Jewish cabal secretly conspiring to control the world is a staple of Islamic anti-Semitism.[101]

As one would expect, translations of the nineteenth-century Russian forgery *The Protocols of the Elders of Zion*, and of Hitler's *Mein Kampf*, are perennial best-sellers in the Muslim Middle East. They are also found for sale in bookstores in London's Muslim neighborhoods. Holocaust denial is equally popular. European Holocaust deniers are welcomed at conferences on the subject regularly held in the Middle East, such as the International Conference on the Palestinian Intifada, held in August 2003, which invited as a speaker Australian-German "revisionist" Fredrick Töben, or the conference hosted by Iran in December 2006, at which former Ku Klux Klan grand wizard David Duke made an appearance along with French Holocaust-denier Robert Faurisson. Given that Muslim anti-Semitism reaches European Muslims through shows like Yusuf al-Qaradawi's program on Al Jazeera—where he regularly rejects any dialogue with the Jews "except for the sword and the rifle"—to attribute Muslim immigrant anti-Semitic attacks to anguish over the predicament of the Palestinians is incredible.[102] Thus, it is not surprising that many European Muslims repeat such invective, like the French Muslim whose father told him, "There will be a final war between Muslims and Jews, and the Jews will be destroyed; it says so in the Qur'an."[103]

Muslim-inspired anti-Semitism, moreover, finds reinforcement not just on the European extreme right but also on the left. Modern anti-Semitism is based on the Jews' embodiment of all the neo-Marxist bogeys such as the dysfunctions and corruption caused by capitalism and liberal democracy, and their alleged money worship and rootless individualism. These days this complaint is associated with all the presumed ills of globalization, that "juggernaut of international corporate finance, Jewish media, and American military power," as one commentator describes the caricature.[104] This theme obviously resonates on the right, which is concerned with the decadence of the West brought about by secularization, the loss of cultural traditions, and the corruption caused by consumer capitalist hedonism. Yet the anti-globalization left also finds a convenient scapegoat in the Jews and Israel, the latter a supposed neo-colonial outpost serving as the minion of international capitalism. "Among those burning the Star of David," Gabriel Schoenfeld writes, "and chanting obscene slogans against the Jewish state in the streets of Europe, there are surely some neo-Nazis, but a greater host of environmentalists, pacifists, anarchists, anti-globalists and socialists."[105] Nor is such anti-Semitic iconography the purview only of the anti-globalization left. In May 2005, Germany's most powerful labor union featured on the cover of its magazine a mosquito in an Uncle Sam top hat, grinning beneath a hooked nose and flashing a gold tooth. The old anti-Semitic trope of the Jew as rich bloodsucker was obvious.[106]

Presumably well-educated European politicians, especially leftists, are also not above indulging old anti-Semitic stereotypes, such as the mythic Jewish powers that allow them to control the world. In England, a Labour M.P. said Tony Blair was "unduly influenced by a cabal of Jewish advisors."[107] In 2002, Germany's former minister of defense attributed President Bush's desire to remove Saddam Hussein to "a powerful—perhaps overly powerful—Jewish lobby." Otto von Habsburg, a member of the European Parliament, has claimed that in the U.S. Defense Department "key positions are held by Jews; the Pentagon is today a Jewish institution." Yet it is criticism of Israel that provides cover for the indulgence of anti-Semitism. The wife of the former president of the European Central Bank, Gretta Duisenberg, who founded an anti-Israeli group called "Stop the Occupation," carried a Palestinian flag in a rally at which were chanted slogans like "Hamas, Hamas, Jews to the gas."[108] While collecting signatures for a petition against "Israeli imperialism," she joked that her object was to collect six million names, an obvious reference to the toll of the Holocaust. In response to Jews protesting her hanging of the flag from the balcony of her home in Amsterdam, she allegedly said that "rich Jews" were responsible for oppressing the Palestinian people.[109] Such prejudice typifies much of European public discourse in the media, as the now-common habit of comparing Israel to Nazi Germany, or the transformation of the Star of David into a symbol of opprobrium on a par with the swastika, both illustrate.

Anti-Semitism among European Muslims, then, is reinforced by the European establishment's willingness to demonize Israel and to disguise prejudice against Jews as anti-Zionism, an attitude notoriously expressed by the French ambassador to England when he blamed all the world's ills on "that shitty little country" Israel.[110] We should mention as well that for European politicians, the growing number of Muslim voters means that the latter are increasingly important in elections. Hence, pandering to Muslim prejudices such as anti-Semitism and hatred of Israel becomes more frequent, as the career of London mayor Ken Livingstone illustrates. The leftist hatred of democratic capitalism, moreover, likewise validates hatred of Jews and Israel, who are cast as the dark engines behind a neo-imperialist globalization. This failure to champion and support Israel, Europe's cultural and spiritual brother, testifies to the crippling self-loathing that encourages the enemies of the West. As Bat Ye'or writes, "By implicitly enlisting in the Arab-Islamic jihad against Israel . . . Europe has effectively jettisoned its values and undermined the roots of its own civilization."[111]

HATING AMERICANS

Anti-Americanism has in the last five years increased significantly in Western Europe. The latest surveys by the Pew Global Attitudes Project show that only in England does a bare majority of people view America favorably (56 percent). In France only 39 percent, in Germany 37 percent, and in Spain 23 percent hold favorable opinions of the United States. Even more telling, in the E.U. countries, 53 percent saw the United States as a threat to world peace equal to Iran and North Korea; in Germany, 48 percent believe the U.S. is a *greater* threat than an Iran ruled by medieval fundamentalists who are actively seeking nuclear weapons. As the Pew Center's Andrew Kohut told Congress, a "feature of contemporary anti-Americanism is that it is no longer just the U.S. as a country that is perceived negatively, but increasingly the American people as well, a sign that anti-American opinions are deepening and becoming more entrenched."[112]

Conventional wisdom lays this decline at the feet of President Bush and the war in Iraq, with its attendant fallout from Abu Ghraib and Guantanamo Bay. Due to the president's policies and style, the vast reservoir of goodwill toward America occasioned by 9/11 was squandered. The sympathy expressed by Jean-Marie Colombani's commentary in *Le Monde*, "We are all Americans," two days after 9/11, was destroyed by the "cowboy" Bush and his preference for unilateral force over multilateral diplomacy. Yet this analysis does not hold up under scrutiny of the historical evidence, which suggests that much of the presumed sympathy was pro forma, if not hypocritical. Even Colombani's sympathy was short-lived. By December 2001, he was describing the United States as the mirror image of the jihadist terrorists and thus responsible for the attacks, and on the first anniversary of 9/11— before the war commenced in Iraq—he wrote in *Le Monde*, "The reflex of solidarity from last year has been deluged by a wave that would have everyone in the world believe we have all become anti-Americans." Similarly, in Germany, defense minister Peter Struck's echo of Colombani on September 12, 2001—"Today we are all

Americans"—was derided by the intelligentsia and approved by only 46 percent of Germans.[113]

The origins of the current outburst of anti-Americanism cannot be completely explained by the president's actions of the last six years. As Andrei Markovits notes, anti-Americanism "hails from a very long and fertile history, and . . . it is only superficially related to the dislike of George W. Bush and his administration's policies. The latter have merely served as convenient caricatures for a much deeper structural disconnect between Europe as an emerging political entity and a new global player, on the one hand, and the United States, its main, perhaps only, genuine rival, on the other. Anti-Americanism in Europe long preceded George W. Bush and will persist long after his departure."[114]

Anti-Americanism, then, is not so much a response to actual behavior or actions, but rather what Paul Hollander calls a "predisposition, a free-floating hostility or aversion," a prejudice "less than fully rational and not necessarily well-founded."[115] This "predisposition," moreover, has as Markovits notes a long history among Europeans: "[A]n era never existed in which European intellectuals and literati—European elites— view the United States without a solid base of resentment, or better, *ressentiment*. Accompanying this resentment, one will usually find envy, jealousy, hatred, denigration, as well as a sense of impotence and repressed revenge."[116] At the start, the United States was despised by aristocratic Europe for its vulgarity, egalitarianism, lack of refinement and culture, and go-getting economic aggression— precisely the stereotypes indulged by today's haters of America. The German Romantic poet Heinrich Heine articulated this disdain when he wrote about sailing to America, "To that pig-pen of Freedom/Inhabited by boors living in equality." After America became a global industrial power in the early twentieth century, it was faulted for its philistine obsession with economic production and regimentation. A German disciple of Nietzsche wrote, "In America, everything is a block, pragmatism, and the national Taylor system," and another decried America's "uninterrupted, exclusive and relentless striving after gain, riches and influence."[117]

Such estimations are typical of the stereotypes that have hardened into European received wisdom on the topic of the United States. Americans are greedy, soulless, obsessed with money and status, power-hungry, and intolerant philistines with no true culture or refinement and no *joie de vivre*. At the same time that Americans are rank materialists, however, they are also repressed religious fanatics, a stereotype reflecting Europe's deep-seated secularization and intolerance of faith. These traditional prejudices became seasoned with envy and resentment after the U.S. twice rescued Europe from its own political nightmares, rebuilt the continent after World War II—spending more than $100 billion in current dollars—and then during the Cold War protected Europe from the Soviet menace. Even more galling for Europeans, this military domination has been accompanied by a global economic, cultural, and linguistic influence far outstripping that of the European nations that once ruled the world. The spectacle of a nation comprising Europe's outcasts dominating and surpassing the mother culture, not to mention occupying the place of global influence rightly due to the cultural superior, is for many Europeans an intolerable humiliation.

Given this long tradition, then, it wasn't George Bush who created the hate-filled and sometimes lunatic statements about America that regularly have issued from European artists, writers, and politicians after 9/11 and the wars in Afghanistan and Iraq. British playwright Harold Pinter used the occasion of accepting his Nobel Prize to say, "The crimes of the United States have been systematic, constant, vicious, remorseless."[118] Novelist Margaret

Drabble fumed, "I loathe the United States and what it has done to Iraq and the rest of the helpless world."[119] The editors of the Swedish paper *Aftonblade*, one week after 9/11, wrote, "The U.S. is the greatest mass murderer of our time"—this from the country that sat out World War II and traded with the *real* champion of mass murder, Nazi Germany. [120] German film director Peter Zadek said, "I deeply detest America," an opinion similar to Greek composer Mikis Theodorokis's "I hate Americans and everything American."[121] The most irrational manifestation of this neurosis, however, was the publication and huge sales of *L'effroyable imposture*, in English *The Big Lie*, which argued that the 9/11 attacks were orchestrated by the U.S. government. Lest you think such bizarre invective is the consequence of post-9/11 U.S. foreign policy, consider that it is in spirit no different from John-Paul Sartre's statement in 1953 that "America is a mad dog."[122]

As such irrational statements show, anti-Americanism is in fact a political religion in Europe, one that unites right and left and thus functions as a unifying belief of pan-European identity. For the left particularly, the success of American democratic capitalism repudiates cherished socialist dogmas. As far back as 1957, Raymond Aron wrote, "The European left has a grudge against the United States mainly because the latter has succeeded by means which were not laid down in the revolutionary code. Prosperity, power, the tendency towards uniformity of economic conditions—these results have been achieved by private initiative, by competition rather than State intervention, in other words by capitalism, which every well-brought-up intellectual has been taught to despise."[123] Yet the post-Marxist complaints against modernity likewise find their target in America, the standard-bearer of all the historical changes that have disturbed European elites for more than two centuries: materialism, standardization, rootlessness, suburbanization, economic ruthlessness, competition, imperial power-hunger, globalization, and all the other old Romantic/post-Marxist charges. British author A. N. Wilson played on these hoary stereotypes in 2002 when he wrote, "They [Americans] are the most merciless exponents of world capitalism, with the determination to have a McDonald's and a Starbucks . . . in every country on earth."[124] Nor are such opinions held only by the elite: European politicians find such prejudices useful in appealing to voters, as Gerhard Schroeder did in 2002, when on the campaign trail he scorned the "American way" and its "plundering of the little man in the United States," or French presidential candidate François Bayrou, who in the spring of 2007 called the United States the "cause of chaos" in the Middle East, and criticized America's "survival of the fittest" economic model.[125]

If these stereotypes sound familiar, it's because they are similar to those that make up modern anti-Semitism. Indeed, many analysts have seen that these two irrational prejudices are "twins," similar manifestations of the same intellectual dysfunction. "Both hatreds," Daniel Johnson writes, "are impervious to the objections of logic or the evidence of history. In both, prejudice functions as a matrix of self-justifying, holistic conspiracy theories that substitute for rational thought. Both rely on fantasies about power and influence, discerning hidden patterns, concocting atrocity stories, gliding over inconvenient disconfirming facts."[126] This convergence of anti-Semitism and anti-Americanism is obvious at every anti-globalization rally: at the 2003 World Economic Forum in Davos, one demonstrator wore a Donald Rumsfeld mask and a huge yellow Star of David, accompanied by a golden calf while being whipped by another demonstrator in an Ariel Sharon mask. As Joseph Joffe noted, "The culprits are now Jews/Israelis and Americans who act as acolytes of Mammon and as avant-garde of pernicious global capitalism."[127]

Both of these prejudices reinforce Europe's most potent political religion, the leftist hatred of free-market capitalism and its utopian fantasies of a world in which freedom, equality, peace, and prosperity can be achieved through the rational techniques of expert elites wielding the coercive power of the state. Such faith, however, flies in the face of the historical evidence that demonstrates the impossibility of achieving these utopian boons, and the bloody disasters that have followed from the attempts to realize them on the part of the passionate believers in this progressive creed. By making such prejudices the unifying force of pan-European identity and defining Europe as the "not-America," Europeans are weakening Western solidarity in the face of an implacable enemy wishing to destroy everything the West stands for.

More importantly, however, these prejudices reinforce and legitimize the hatred of the West rampant throughout the Muslim world, for all the ills of the West find their highest and most powerful embodiment in the United States. This hatred was visible after 9/11 in the at best ambivalent, at worst celebratory comments about the murders in Manhattan. The words of a Saudi cleric published in a London Arabic-language newspaper say it all: "I will not conceal from you [the letter is addressed to President Bush] that a tremendous wave of joy accompanied the shock that was felt by Muslims in the street."[128] Of course, this pleasure at America's suffering was expressed by European haters of America as well: "How we have dreamt of this event," French philosopher Jean Baudrillard wrote after 9/11, "how the whole world has dreamt of it because nobody could fail to dream of the destruction of any power that has become hegemonic."[129]

Muslim anti-Americanism has many sources, not the least being the traditional Islamic disdain for the infidel. But the complaints of the jihadists are often very similar to those of European America-haters, and spring from the same resentment of a global power that stands in the way of European or jihadist ambitions.

Muslim Brotherhood theorist Sayyid Qutb, after his two years in America, "saw the West as a gigantic brothel, steeped in animal lust, greed, and selfishness."[130] The theme of America as the chief global-capitalist exploiter was sounded as well in Osama bin Laden's "Letter to America" published in November 2002, in which he called the United States "the worst civilization witnessed by the history of mankind," a sentiment shared by many Europeans, who no doubt would also agree with bin Laden's claim that America's "law is the law of the rich and wealthy people, who hold sway in their political parties, and fund their election campaigns with their gifts. Behind them stand the Jews, who control your policies, media and economy."[131] Such beliefs are daily repeated in the mainstream Middle Eastern media, most of it government-controlled, usually spiced up with the traditional anti-Semitic slanders also used by the European anti-globalization left.[132]

An anti-Americanism that validates the hallucinatory fantasies of the jihadist enemy is of course a suicidal indulgence, for the jihadists hate Europe for the same reasons they hate the United States. As such, anti-Americanism is another sign of Eurabian appeasement, an attempt to placate Muslim immigrants at home and buy off the jihadists by attacking the power that is actively resisting their assaults on the West. "The demonization of America by anti-Americanism," James Ceaser writes, "not only calls into question the community of interests between Europe and America but threatens the idea of the West. It pulls the various pieces of the West apart and sets them at war with one another. Theoretical anti-Americanism is the Trojan horse that has been introduced to destroy Western civilization."[133]

Recently, some European nations have started to change course in their expectations for Muslim Europeans. Radical Muslim preachers are being deported, mosques notorious for preaching violence are being surveilled, immigration and assimilation policies are being strengthened, Islamic practices that contradict Western custom, such as the veil and headscarf, are being restricted in public. Many European thinkers have bravely protested against attempts to restrict foundational rights such as free speech, including some Muslims like Danish member of parliament Naser Khader, whom a radical imam has threatened to blow up, or London *Times* columnist Murad Ahmed, who has called jihadists "nutcases."[134] Yet the multicultural attitudes that empower Muslim immigrant separation from the mores and cultures of their host countries are deep-seated and widely dispersed throughout public institutions such as the courts, media, and schools. And the reflex of self-loathing and guilt over presumed Western crimes and dysfunctions inhibits the defensive pride necessary to meet and defeat these serious challenges to the Western way.[135]

Moreover, their still exists a very real danger of more terrorist attacks like the bombings in London and Madrid. England's domestic intelligence agency, MI5, is keeping under surveillance sixteen hundred suspects in two hundred terrorist cells. Thirty conspiracies are currently under investigation, and in August 2006 British intelligence foiled a plot to blow up several airliners en route from Heathrow to the United States.[136] Equally frightening are the opinion polls that reveal high levels of support for violence among European Muslims. England's ICM polling service found in February 2006 that 13 percent of British Muslims believe it is right "to exercise violence against those who are deemed by religious leaders to have insulted them"—that's more than two hundred thousand people.[137] In June 2006, the Pew Global Attitudes Project revealed that among French, Spanish, and British Muslims, from one-fourth to a third "sometimes" or "rarely" supported suicide bombers.[138] That they do so at all rather than unequivocally condemning such murder speaks volumes about the sentiments of "moderate" European Muslims. Given that it took only nineteen terrorists to bring down the World Trade Center towers and murder almost three thousand people, these are alarming numbers of potential terrorists and terrorist sympathizers.

In the past, Europe's resistance to Islamic imperial ambition was fired by Christian faith. When the last Islamic military threat to the West was turned back at Vienna in September 1683, the Polish general Count Sobieski told his troops, "It is not a city alone that we have to save, but the whole of Christianity, of which the city of Vienna is the bulwark. The war is a holy one." "The men from Warsaw crossed themselves," Paul Fregosi writes, "shouted hurrah, praised the Lord of hosts and prepared to fight and die for God, for the Black Virgin of Czestochowa, for Poland, and maybe a bit for Vienna too."[139] But having abandoned God and country, where will Europe find the spiritual resources to assert the rightness of the Western civilization Christianity helped to create, and fight back vigorously against those who wish to destroy it?

FOUR

■■■■■

THE ROAD TO NOWHERE

EVEN THE MOST ardent champions of EUtopia acknowledge
that the problems outlined in this book are serious challenges
for Europe's future. At the end of his pæan to the "European
Dream," even Jeremy Rifkin frets that Europeans' "personal sense
of accountability and responsibility is not deep enough" to meet
these challenges, and he worries whether their "sense of hope is
sufficient to the task of sustaining a new vision for the future."[1]
Overregulated, economics; unsustainable lavish social-welfare
entitlements; aging and dwindling populations; and growing
numbers of unassimilated, sullen immigrants are the four vectors
that in the future may converge with disastrous consequences for
the European Dream.[2]

Many European politicians acknowledge these challenges, but
institutional inertia and resistance to change hamstring their
attempts to correct them. Angela Merkel was elected Germany's
chancellor in 2005 on a platform of economic reform, yet her
"policy of small steps" has so far done little to address the deep-
seated structural problems causing Germany's economic ills. Likewise in France, Nicolas Sarkozy was elected president in 2007 on
the strength of promises to free up France's sclerotic economy and

address the festering problems of underemployed and lawless Muslim immigrants. But given the vehemence of the protests in March 2006 against mild reforms to hiring and firing regulations, it seems unlikely that Sarkozy can undertake the more serious changes that can meet the economic challenges facing France. As for the greater foreign policy challenge of Islamic jihad, the fate of England's Tony Blair—who left the prime minister's office discredited by his support of America's war against jihad in Iraq—is a warning to other European politicians that significant numbers of their people do not have the stomach for that fight.

Nor does the E.U. show any evidence of being the institutional mechanism that will be able to deal with these problems. Many Europeans themselves don't think so: in 2005, the French and the Dutch rejected the five-hundred-page European Constitution, putting the whole project on hold for the present. A 2006 poll found that less than half of E.U. populations thought their membership in the E.U. was a "good thing," a number nearly identical to those who believe the E.U. is "going in the right direction."[3] In March 2007, the fifty-year anniversary celebration of the Treaty of Rome, which began the process of European integration, was "shadowed by a sense that the union is stuck in something like a midlife crisis—unhappy about its divided present, uncertain about what path to take in the future," according to *The New York Times*.[4] Former German foreign minister Joschka Fischer, an ardent champion of a European federal government, was more blunt: "The E.U. is on autopilot, in stalemate, in deep crisis."[5]

This crisis stems from the utopian ambitions of the E.U., its dream to transcend nationalism, marginalize religious faith, and create peace and prosperity through international agreements and rational techniques wielded by experts—the Enlightenment dream that for the past two centuries has facilitated the various bloody pseudo-religions discussed earlier. To transcend nationalism, moreover, begs the question whether nationalism and the nation state *can* or *should* be transcended.[6] Nor has the excesses of fascist nationalism, the rationale for E.U. postnationalism, discredited nationalism per se. "It is inhuman," Alain Finkielkraut writes, "to define man by blood and soil but no less inhuman to leave him stumbling through life with the terrestrial foundations of his existence taken out from under him."[7]

Philosophical issues aside, if we look just to the practical behavior of many European states, national self-interest, and *amour propre* are more potent motivators of state action than are the abstract ideals of the E.U. Economic protectionism, most obvious in the agricultural subsidies that consume 40 percent of the E.U. budget, is just one example of how the interests of the nation take priority over those of "Europe." The failure to create the much heralded, but militarily modest, European Rapid Reaction Force is another example of how national priorities trump the E.U.'s. Given high social-welfare costs and pacifist inclinations, individual nations simply cannot or will not spend the money necessary to create a shared military capability that can project force in the world and thus wield international clout commensurate with Europe's pretensions to be a global power that can "balance" that of the United States. Time will tell whether repressed nationalist and patriotic sentiments, under pressure from Islamic aggression, will return in xenophobic or neo-fascist form. But the conflict within the E.U. transnational ideal—the self-interested economic and political behavior of individual states, and the repressed or denigrated feelings of patriotic pride and national belonging—will itself continue to be a problem in European life.

Finally, neither the E.U. nor European governments appear willing to take the steps necessary to counter the threat of jihadist terrorism, relying on surveillance and investigation instead of addressing the root problems caused by lax immigration controls,

the failure to demand and facilitate assimilation, and the appeasement of immigrant dysfunction. And the threat of more terrorist
attacks remains very real: in late June 2007, a plot to detonate car
bombs in London and an attack on the Glasgow airport both failed
only because of the incompetence of the terrorists. Interfaith "dialogue" and reactive police work are no more likely than sheer luck
to prevent the next attack.

All these problems, however, reflect the larger issue that lies at
the heart of this book's argument: the lack of a unifying belief and
set of values that can substitute for an abandoned Christianity,
and a corrosive doubt about the greatness and achievements of
the West.[8] From the beginning, the E.U. was troubled by a failure
to articulate "what principle lay behind the arrangement and how
far this common undertaking was to go."[9] Currently, being "not-
America" seems to be the most powerful force uniting Europeans,
but this irrational prejudice cannot in the long term hold together
such disparate peoples and traditions in the teeth of such serious
challenges. For one thing, anti-Americanism is concentrated in
"Old Europe," while the newer members of the E.U. from Eastern
Europe, such as Poland, are more friendly to the nation that took
the lead in liberating them from the Soviet yoke. More importantly, Europeans run the risk of alienating the American people,
who might finally tire of Europe's taking a free security ride at
America's expense and begin to question the need of organizations like NATO, the bulk of whose funding and equipment
comes from the United States. An E.U. that cannot on its own
protect its member states from aggression will quickly collapse.[10]

If pride in the nation and belief in its unifying identity are
abandoned, if the future is a matter of indifference for the child-
less, and most important, if traditional Christianity is discarded,
what values, ideals, beliefs will then unify Europeans? Having cut
itself off from the Christian tradition that helped to create all the

ideals Europe professes to respect—human rights, equality, tolerance, separation of church and state, respect for individuals, to
name a few—how long can Europe live off what Christopher
Dawson called "the accumulated capital of its Christian past, from
which it drew the moral and social idealism that inspired the
humanitarian and liberal and democratic movements of the last
two centuries"?[11] Faced with an enemy that knows passionately
what is worth dying and killing for, what will Europe, devoted to
material pleasure and riddled with self-doubt, die and kill for? A
shorter workweek, early retirement, Internet pornography, state-
funded abortion, afternoon adultery, the whole *dolce vita* lifestyle
constantly held up as a reproach to us money-grubbing, workaholic, overreligious Americans?

None of these material goods is worth dying for. Rather, each
is negotiable, a bargaining chip easily given up for physical comfort, temporary security, and one more day of life. In the long
term, however, this tradeoff is nothing other than a form of slow-
motion suicide.

Acknowledgements

Thanks are due to Roger Kimball and all the folks at Encounter Books for their support and encouragement. Victor Davis Hanson as always was generous with his advice and friendship. My wife Jacalyn read the manuscript and in general put up with me. Finally, this book was made possible by the generous support of the Harvey L. Karp Foundation.

Notes

Chapter 1: The Road to EUtopia

1 Christopher Dawson, *The Making of Europe* (1932; rpt. Washington, D.C., 2003), 15.
2 In *American Vertigo* (New York, 2006), 135.
3 In *Menace in Europe* (New York, 2006), 15-16. Krugman's column appeared 29 July 2005.
4 In Timothy Garton Ash, "The New Anti-Europeanism in America," in *Beyond Paradise and Power*, ed. Tod Lindberg (New York and London, 2005), 126.
5 In *Free World* (New York, 2004), 65.
6 See T. R. Reid, *The United States of Europe*, 167–71; Carlo Ciampi quoted by Peter Finn, *Washington Post* (18 January 2003); in Joseph Joffe, *Überpower* (New York, 2006), 80.
7 *New York Times* (27 December 2005).
8 *New York Times* (19 November 2006).
9 Tony Judt, *Postwar* (New York, 2005), 789.
10 See Joffe, *Überpower*, 98–104.
11 *The Economist* (24 December 2005–6 January 2006), 76.
12 *Postwar*, 730–31.
13 See Judt's description of this divide in *Postwar*, 757.
14 In Tony Blankley, *The West's Last Chance* (Washington, D.C., 2005), 153–54.
15 In Jeremy Rifkin, *The European Dream* (New York, 2004), 211.
16 *New York Times* (4 December 2005).
17 Anne Applebaum, "'Old Europe' vs. 'New Europe,'" in *Beyond Paradise and Power*, 30.
18 William Shawcross, *Allies* (New York, 2005), 185.
19 Kenneth R. Timmerman, *The French Betrayal of America* (New York, 2005), 249.
20 In *Of Paradise and Power* (New York, 2004), 3.
21 See Andrei S. Markovits, *Uncouth Nation* (Princeton, 2007), 84–85.
22 In *Postwar*, 69.
23 Judt, *Postwar*, 353.
24 In Robert J. Leiber, *The American Era* (Cambridge, 2005), 66–67.
25 *Paradise and Power*, 3.
26 Mark Leonard, *Why Europe Will Run the 21st Century* (London and New York, 2005), 143.

27 In *The European Dream*, 3, 8; Postwar, 800.

28 Kalypso Nicolaidis, "The Power of the Superpowerless," in *Beyond Paradise and Power*, 97, 103, 105.

29 In *Free World*, 47–48.

30 In Joffe, *Überpower*, 118.

31 *Free World*, 47–48; emphases in original.

32 Nicolaidis, "The Power of the Superpowerless," 105.

33 *The United States of Europe*, 146.

34 *The Definitive Time Machine*, ed. Harry M. Geduld (1884; Bloomington and Indianapolis, 1987), 57.

35 *The Time Machine*, 45, 46, 48, 49, 68.

36 In John J. Miller and Mark Molesky, *Our Oldest Enemy* (New York, 2004), 242.

37 *Free World*, 96.

38 Samantha Powers, *A Problem from Hell* (New York, 2002), 277.

39 *The American Era*, 81.

40 *Free World*, 96.

41 Lieber, *The American Era*, 85–86.

42 *Allies*, 85.

43 Of *Paradise and Power*, 47–48.

44 *Postwar*, 684.

45 Reported by Jeffrey Gedmin, U.S. director of the Aspen Institute in Berlin, in *Allies*, 124.

46 *The French Betrayal of America*, 19.

47 See *Allies*, 100–4.

48 *The French Betrayal of America*, 39.

49 *Allies*, 92–93. Cf. *The French Betrayal of America*, 46.

50 See *French Betrayal of America*, 39–49

51 *French Betrayal of America*, 114, 52.

52 *The American Era*, 149; David Pryce-Jones, *Betrayal* (New York, 2006), 142.

53 *French Betrayal of America*, 189, 191.

54 Pryce-Jones, *Betrayal*, 142.

55 *Allies*, 99.

56 Of *Paradise and Power*, 37.

57 Cf. Joffe, *Überpower*, 168: "E.U.-Europe devotes 1.9 percent of domestic output to its military, which is half the American ration and about one-half of U.S. spending in absolute terms." Moreover, the Europeans spend half as much on modernizing their equipment, and 50 percent more on personnel (*The Economist* [25 February 2006], 59).

58 In *Our Oldest Enemy*, 45–46.

59 *Austerlitz*, trans. Anthea Bell (New York, 2001), 123.

60 *Austerlitz*, 103, 6.

61 *Platform*, trans. Frank Wynne (New York, 2002), 152.

62 *Platform*, 18, 45, 183.

63 *Platform*, 191.

64 *Platform*, 213.

65 *Platform*, 258.

66 In "The Defeaticrats," *National Review* (31 December 2005), 31.

67 In *The American Enterprise* (October–December 2005), 23.

68 European suicide rates: World Health Organization, *Suicide Prevention in Europe* (2002), 1. American: National Institute for Mental Health, *In Harm's Way: Suicide in America* (2003).

69 Joel Kotkin, "American Still Beckons," *The American Enterprise* (October-December 2005), 30; see too the April 2006 issue, 7.

70 The European Citizens and the Future of Europe, May 2006 (http://ec.europa.eu/public_opinion/quali/ql_futur_en.pdf).

71 *New York Times* (25 July 2006).

CHAPTER 2: THE DEATH OF GOD
AND SOME FAILING GODS

1 John Keegan, *The First World War* (New York, 1999), 10.

2 David Fromkin, *Europe's Last Summer* (New York, 2004), 13.

3 Fromkin, 5.

4 Keegan, *The First World War*, 423.

5 In Fromkin, 6.

6 In *The Cube and the Cathedral* (New York, 2005), 23.

7 Weigel, 40, 41.

8 Rifkin, 20-21.

9 In Brian C. Anderson, *Democratic Capitalism and Its Discontents* (Wilmington, DE, 2007), 49.

10 *The United States of Europe*, 215–216.

11 *The West's Last Chance*, 155.

12 Cf. Judt's comments on Spain, 774.

13 George Weigel, "Europe's Two Culture Wars," *Commentary* (May 2006), 30, 31.

14 Berlinski, 62–63.

15 Melanie Phillips, *Londonistan* (New York, 2006), 141.

16 Weigel, "Europe's Two Culture Wars," 36.

NOTES

17 *The Cube and the Cathedral*, 19–20.

18 *The Cube and the Cathedral*, 58–59.

19 See *The Cube and the Cathedral*, 159–61.

20 *Christianity and the Crisis of Cultures* (San Francisco, 2005), 44–45.

21 Berlinski, 62.

22 *The Gay Science*, trans. Walter Kaufmann (New York, 1974), 167, 279; *The Will to Power*, in Henri de Lubac, *The Drama of Atheist Humanism*, 7th ed. (San Francisco, 1983), 116.

23 *The Gay Science*, 181.

24 *The Secularization of the European Mind in the 19th Century* (1975; Oxford, 1990), 17.

25 In "Montesquieu," *Against the Current*, ed. Henry Hardy (New York, 1980), 5–6.

26 *Reflections on the Revolution in France*, in Burleigh, *Earthly Powers*, 43.

27 *The Captive Mind*, trans. Jane Zielonko (1955; New York, 1990), 73.

28 *The Enlightenment: The Rise of Modern Paganism* (New York, 1966), 149.

29 *The Secularization of the European Mind in the 19th Century*, 156.

30 *Earthly Powers*, 81.

31 *The Passing of an Illusion*, trans. Deborah Furet (1995; Chicago, 1999), 32.

32 *Thus Spoke Zarathustra*, trans. R. J. Hollingdale (London, 1961), 297.

33 In *Freedom and Its Betrayal*, ed. Henry Hardy (Princeton, N.J., 2002), 108.

34 *Earthly Powers*, 230.

35 In *The Drama of Atheist Humanism*, 251, 149.

36 In *Earthly Powers*, 215.

37 In *The Secularization of the European Mind*, 166.

38 In *The Secularization of the European Mind*, 171.

39 The phrase "evangelical atheism" from Jennifer Michael Hecht, *The End of the Soul* (New York, 2003).

40 For a fuller discussion see Michael Burleigh, *Sacred Causes* (New York, 2007), 38–122.

41 *The Old Regime and the French Revolution*, in Burleigh, *Earthly Powers*, 92.

42 In Burleigh, *Earthly Powers*, 9.

43 Furet, *The Passing of an Illusion*, 181.

44 Furet, 31.

45 Richard Pipes, *Communism. A History* (New York, 2001), 103–4; Furet, 191.

46 *The Anatomy of Fascism* (New York, 2004), 41.

47 In *Sacred Causes*, 105.

48 *The Economist* (27 May 2006), 48.

49 *The New York Times*, 13 July 2006.

50 *The New York Times*, 14 December 2006.

51 See the figures for individual European countries at
    http://www.irr.org.uk/europe/.

52 Paxton, 186.

53 *Free World*, 197–98.

54 *The Anatomy of Fascism*, 174.

55 In *The Extreme Right in Western Europe* (Manchester and New York, 2005),
    37.

56 *Earthly Powers*, 14–15.

57 See Jocelyn Cesari, *When Islam and Democracy Meet* (2004; New York,
    2006), 33.

58 She Olivier Guitta, "The Veil Controversy," *The Weekly Standard* (4 December 2006), 16.

59 Anthony Daniels, "Liberté, Egalité, Colonialisme," *National Review* (31
    December 2005), 28.

60 In Jytte Klausen, *The Islamic Challenge* (Oxford, 2005), 124. Spain: Christopher Caldwell, "Europe's Future," *The Weekly Standard* (4 December 2006),
    25.

61 *The New York Times* (2 October 2006).

62 *The New York Times* (28 February 2006).

63 *Menace in Europe*, 180.

64 *Menace in Europe*, 225; 204, emphasis in original; 230.

65 In *Occidentalism*, Ian Buruma and Avishai Margulit (New York, 2004), 54;
    Qutb 119–121.

66 For data on latest elections, go to www.europeangreens.org.

67 Andrew Dobson, *Green Political Thought*, 3rd edition (London and New
    York, 2000), 8.

68 Dobson, 11.

69 *Green Political Thought*, 19.

70 Document available at www.global.greens.org.au/charter2001pdf.

71 Document available at
    ec.europa.eu/comm/development/body/tmp_docs/europan_council_
    conclusions_en_15_1.

72 *The Real Environmental Crisis* (Berkeley and London, 2003), 2.

73 In *DNA: The Secret of Life* (New York, 2003), 150.

74 In *Landscape and Memory* (New York, 1995), 119.

75 Janet Biehl, in *Ecofascism* (Edinburgh and San Francisco, 1995), 39.

76 *Ecofascism*, 35.

77 Stephanie Courtois et al., *The Black Book of Communism*, trans. Mark Kramer
    and Jonathon Murphy (Cambridge, Mass., 1999).

78 For the most recent statistics, see www.ulb.ac.be/soco/cevipol.html.

79 *Koba the Dread* (New York, 2002), 257.

80 "The myth of the Left presupposes the myth of progress," Raymond Aron,
    The Opium of the Intellectuals (1957; New Brunswick, N.J., 2001), 94.

81 In Amis, 85.

82 See Furet, 26.

83 *The Drama of Atheist Humanism*, 136.

84 Muravchik, *Heaven on Earth*, 55–56.

85 De Lubac, *Drama of Atheist Humanism*, 39.

86 Pipes, *Communism*, 12.

87 De Lubac, 37.

88 Muravchik, 37.

89 *Earthly Powers*, 244.

90 In Chadwick, 76.

91 In Muravchik, 60.

92 *Heavenly Powers*, 250.

93 See Furet, 67.

94 *The Captive Mind*, 133.

95 Chadwick, 64.

96 In Muravchik, 343.

97 *The Drama of Atheist Humanism*, 434.

98 In Pipes, 68.

99 *The Drama of Atheist Humanism*, 436.

100 In *The God That Failed*, ed. Richard H. Crossman (1950; New York, 2001),
    173.

101 In *The God That Failed*, 17, 23.

102 Lewis S. Feuer, *Ideology and the Ideologues*, in Robert Conquest, *Reflections on
    a Ravaged Century* (New York, 2001), 44.

103 Pipes, 148–49.

104 In *Reflections on a Ravaged Century*, 53.

105 In Paul Johnson, *Intellectuals* (New York, 1988), 71.

106 Pipes, 68.

107 In Conquest, *Reflections on a Ravaged Century*, 98.

108 Furet, 79; cf. also 138.

109 Muravchik, 136.

110 Amis, 30, 29.

111 Pipes, 73–74.

112 Furet, 83.

113 Furet, 106.

114 Furet, 114.

NOTES

115 Furet, 146.

116 *In Denial* (San Francisco, 2003), 8.

117 Karl Zinsmeister and Olaf Gersemann, "Europe's Declining Vigor," *The American Enterprise* (October–December 2005), 20.

118 Data available from the Organization for Economic Cooperation and Development, www.oecdwash.org./DATA/online.htm.

119 See the data in Guillermo de la Dehesa, *Europe at the Crossroads* (New York, 2006).

120 In "Europe's Not Working," *The American Enterprise* (October–December 2005), 27.

121 In "Revolting in France," *The Weekly Standard* (1 May 2006), 32.

122 In *The United States of Europe*, 172.

123 In *The American Enterprise* (October–December 2006), 23.

124 In F. A. Hayek, *The Road to Serfdom* (1944; Chicago, 1994), 29.

125 *Without Roots*, 78.

126 Melanie Phillips, *Londonistan* (New York, 2006), 117, 120, 123.

127 *In My Country Right or Left*, ed. Sonia Orwell and Ian Angus (New York, 1968), 15.

128 In *The Tragic Sense of Life*, trans. J. E. Crawford Flitch (1921; New York, 1954), 27.

129 In *Christianity and European Culture*, ed. Gerald J. Russello (Washington, D.C., 1990), 78.

130 In "Troubled Continent," *The National Review* (13 February 2006), 36–37.

131 *Without Roots*, 33.

132 epp.eurostat.cec.eu.int/pls/portal/docs/PAGE/PGP_PRD_CAT_ PREREL/PGE_CAT_PR

133 Denise Owen Harrigan, *Maxwell Perspective* (Fall 2003).

134 Philip Longman, *The Empty Cradle* (New York, 2004), 63.

135 Steyne, *America Alone*, 10.

136 epp.eurostat.cec.eu.int/pls/portal/docs/PAGE/PGP_PRD_CAT_ PREREL/PGE_CAT_PR

137 Elisabeth Rosenthal, *The New York Times* (22 September 2006).

138 Longman, *The Empty Cradle*, 63.

139 *Europe at the Crossroads*, 85.

140 *The Cube and the Cathedral*, 164.

141 See Longman's discussion, *The Empty Cradle*, 33–36.

142 *America Alone* xix.

CHAPTER 3: EURABIA

1 *The Camp of the Saints*, trans. Norman Shapiro (1975; Petoskey, Mich, 1987), 27, 119, 121.

2 See Christopher Caldwell, "Europe's Future," *The Weekly Standard* (4 December 2006).

3 *While Europe Slept*, 29.

4 *Londonistan*, 20–21.

5 In *The Economist* (3 June 2006), 50.

6 *The Wall Street Journal* (11 November 2005).

7 Jocelyne Cesari, *When Islam and Democracy Meet* (New York, 2004), 23.

8 Flemming Rose, "Europe's Politics of Victimology," RealClearPolitics (www.realclearpolitics.com/articles/2006/05/europes_politics-of-victimology.html).

9 "Should He Have Spoken?" *The New Criterion* 25 (September 2006). Available at www.newcriterion.com/archives/author/rscruton.

10 Bawer, *While Europe Slept*, 29–30.

11 *Menace in Europe*, 46–47.

12 See *The New York Times* (18 December 2005).

13 Rifkin, *The European Dream*, 249.

14 *The Economist*, 24 June 2006, 11.

15 *The Local*, 14 December 2005, http://www.thelocal.se/2683/; Bruce Bawer, "While Sweden Slept," *The New York Sun*, 8 December 2006 (www.nysun.com/article/44831).

16 *While Europe Slept*, 39.

17 "The Barbarians at the Gates of Paris," in *Our Culture, What's Left of It* (Chicago, 2005), 301, 306.

18 *The New York Times*, 21 October 2006.

19 See *While Europe Slept*, 209–211.

20 In *Murder in Amsterdam* (New York, 2006), 234.

21 "Barbarians at the Gates of Paris," in *Our Culture, What's Left of It*, 297.

22 *The New York Times* (21 October 2006).

23 "Looking Around," *National Review* (20 November 2006), 56.

24 In "The Suicide Bombers Among Us," *City Journal* (Autumn 2005), available at www.city-journal.org/printable.php?id=1885.

25 *Eurabia* (Madison and Teaneck, N.J., 2005), 9.

26 *Eurabia*, 10.

27 *Eurabia*, 147.

28 *Eurabia*, 163.

29 See *Eurabia*, 165–67.

30 In *The Legacy of Jihad*, ed. Andrew Bostom (Amherst, 2005), 60.

31 In Ronni L. Gordon and David M. Stillman, "Prince Charles of Arabia," *Middle East Quarterly* (September 1997). Available at www.meforum.org/article/356.

32 In *Londonistan*, 67–68.

33 Klausen, *The Islamic Challenge*, 188.

34 In Oriana Fallaci, *The Force of Reason* (New York, 2004), 56.

35 In *A Heart Turned East*, Adam Lebor (New York, 1998), 122.

36 In Brendan Bernhard, "The Fallaci Code," *LA Weekly* (15 March 2006).

37 *Eurabia*, 98.

38 In Alain Finkielkraut, *The Defeat of the Mind*, trans. Judith Friedlander (1987; New York, 1995), 105.

39 *Eurabia*, 98, 161.

40 In *While Europe Slept*, 30.

41 In *The Discourse on Inequality*, 1755, trans. Julia Conaway Bondarella (New York, 1988), 4.

42 In *The Conquest of Granada*, Part I, Act I, Scene 1.

43 Conversations with Eckermann, in *The Tears of the White Man*, trans. William R. Beer (1983; New York, 1986), 100.

44 Finkielkraut, *The Defeat of the Mind*, 56.

45 See Leszek Kolakowski, *Main Currents of Marxism*, trans. P. S. Falla (New York, 2005), 156–57.

46 See Leszek Kolakowski, "What Is Left of Socialism?" reprint in *My Correct Views on Everything*, ed. Zbigniew Janowski (South Bend, 2005), 92–93.

47 In Stephen Schwartz, *From West to East* (New York, 1998), 82.

48 Kolakowski, *Main Currents of Marxism*, 750–51.

49 In *The Wretched of the Earth*, trans. Richard Philcox (1963; New York, 2004), xiv.

50 *The Strange Death of Marxism* (Columbia and London, 2005), 23, 119.

51 *The Tears of the White Man*, trans. William R. Beer (1983; New York, 1986), 4.

52 *The Wretched of the Earth*, xiv.

53 *The Defeat of the Mind*, 107.

54 Bawer, *While Europe Slept*, 57.

55 George Weigel, "Europe's Two Culture Wars," 32–33.

56 Cesari, *When Islam and Democracy Meet*, 69–70.

57 See Diana West, "Imposing Islamic Law," *The Washington Times* (23 February 2007).

58 Efraim Karsh and Rory Miller, "Europe's Persecuted Muslims?" *Commentary* (April 2007), 53.

59 Daniel Pipes, "Trouble in Londonistan," *The New York Sun* (11 July 2006).

60 *The Islamic Challenge*, 87.

61 In *The Islamic Challenge*, 57.

62 *Londonistan*, 73. As Bruce Bawer reports (*While Europe Slept*, 207), a commission report in Sweden regarding high levels of immigrant crime in Malmö came to the same conclusion: racism was to blame.

63 *The Islamic Challenge*, 58.

64 In *Londonistan*, 53–54.

65 *While Europe Slept*, 225.

66 *Londonistan*, 121, 172–73.

67 In *While Europe Slept*, 162.

68 In *Menace in Europe*, 24–25, 30–31. On Jahjah, see also Klausen, *The Islamic Challenge*, 46.

69 In Fallaci, *The Rage and the Pride*, 36.

70 *While Europe Slept*, 61–63.

71 Robert J. Lieber, *The American Era*, 74.

72 *Londonistan*, 13–15, quote xi.

73 *Londonistan*, 10–11. See too Cesari, *When Islam and Democracy Meet*, 100–109.

74 *Menace in Europe*, 30.

75 Buruma, *Murder in Amsterdam*, 211–213, quote on 212.

76 *Murder in Amsterdam*, 189–90.

77 *Murder in Amsterdam*, 198.

78 *Menace in Europe*, 29.

79 *While Europe Slept*, 195–98.

80 From a speech delivered 27 April 2007; available at http://pewforum.org/events/index.php?EventID=107.

81 See Oriana Fallaci, *The Force of Reason*, 25.

82 *While Europe Slept*, 215.

83 Paul Marshall, "The Mohammed Cartoons," *The Weekly Standard* (13 February 2006), 14.

84 George Weigel, "Europe's Two Culture Wars," 33–34.

85 In *The New York Times* (19 February 2006).

86 Henrik Bering, "The U.N. Plays with Lego," *The Weekly Standard* (3 April 2006), 16.

87 In *The New York Times* (8 February 2006).

88 See http://www.state.gov/g/drl/rls/40258.htm.

89 *The New York Times* (5 March 2006); Nidra Poller, "The Murder of Ilan Halimi," *The Wall Street Journal* (26 February 2006), available at www.opinionjournal.com/extra/?id=110008006&ojrss=wsj.

Notes

90 Details in *Betrayal*, 13.

91 See Efraim Karsh and Rory Miller, "Europe's Persecuted Muslims?" *Commentary* (April 2007), 52.

92 *Postwar*, 775.

93 In John Rosenthal, "Anti-Semitism and Ethnicity in Europe," *Policy Review* (October–November 2003). Available at www.hover.org/publications/policyreview/3446931.html.

94 In *The New Antisemitism* (New York, 2006), 8.

95 *The New York Times* (12 March 2007).

96 Sura 2.61, 5.60 (available at www.quranbrowser.com). See Andrew Bostom, *The Legacy of Islamic Antisemitism* (Amherst, N.Y.: 2007).

97 George Michael, *The Enemy of My Enemy* (Lawrence, Kansas, 2006), 112.

98 *The Enemy of My Enemy*, 116–19.

99 *The Enemy of My Enemy*, 121–23, 125–28.

100 In Gabriel Schoenfeld, *The Return of Anti-Semitism* (San Francisco, 2004), 39–44.

101 In Schoenfeld, *The Return of Anti-Semitism*, 13, 17, 20–21.

102 In *The Changing Face of Antisemitism*, 199.

103 In *Betrayal*, 13.

104 Michael Reynolds, "Virtual Reich," *Playboy* (February 2002). In George Michael, *The Enemy of My Enemy*, 131.

105 *The Return of Anti-Semitism*, 86.

106 In Markovits, *Uncouth Nation*, 161.

107 *The Return of Anti-Semitism*, 95.

108 In "Anti-Semitism and Ethnicity in Europe," 10.

109 *The Return of Anti-Semitism*, 88.

110 In *Betrayal*, 149.

111 *Eurabia*, 115.

112 Data and Kohut's testimony available at http://pewglobal.org/commentary/display.php?AnalysisID=1019; German poll numbers at http://www.spiegel.de/international/germany/0,1518,474636,00.html.

113 Markovits, *Uncouth Nation*, 129–30.

114 *Uncouth Nation*, 16.

115 In *Anti-Americanism: Critiques at Home and Abroad, 1965–1990* (Oxford, 1992), 7.

116 *Uncouth Nation*, 39.

117 In James Ceaser, "The Philosophical Origins of Anti-Amerianism in Europe," 53–54. In Paul Hollander, ed., *Understanding Anti-Americanism* (Chicago, 2004).

118 In Daniel Johnson, "America and the America-Haters," *Commentary* (June 2006), 29.

119 In Lieber, *The American Era*, 196.

120 Bawer, *While Europe Slept*, 79.

121 Zadek in Markovits, *Uncouth Nation*, 25; Theodorokis in Lieber, *The American Era*, 196.

122 In Bruckner, *Tears of the White Man*, 14.

123 *The Opium of the Intellectuals*, 227.

124 In Joffe, *Überpower*, 83.

125 Schroeder in *Überpower*, 83; Bayrou in *The New York Times* (8 March 2007).

126 "America and the America-Haters," 30.

127 *Überpower*, 90–91.

128 In "Anti-Americanism in the Middle East," Patrick Clawson and Barry Rubin. *In Understanding Anti-Americanism*, 125.

129 In *Überpower*, 92. See Markovits, 129–130, for other examples.

130 Ian Baruma and Avishai Margalit, *Occidentalism*, 117.

131 Full text available at http://observer.guardian.co.uk/worldview/story/0,11581,845725,00.html.

132 See the examples collected by Joseph Joffe in *Überpower*, 77–79.

133 "The Philosophical Origins of Anti-Americanism in Europe," 63.

134 See Andrew Stuttaford, "Democratic Muslims," *The National Review* (22 May 2006), 22. Ahmed's column available at http://www.timesonline.co.uk/tol/comment/columnists/guest_contributors/article1329403.ece

135 See the remarks of Islamic scholar Bernard Lewis in the *Jerusalem Post* (29 January 2007); Available at http://www.jpost.com/servlet/Satellite?pagename=JPost%2FJPArticle%2FShowFull&cid=1167467834546.

136 *The New York Times* (23 March 2007).

137 Available at http://www.icmresearch.co.uk/reviews/2006/Sunday%20Telegraph%20%20Mulims%20Feb/Sunday%20Telegraph%20Muslims%20feb06.asp.

138 Available at http://pewglobal.org/reports/display.php?ReportID=253.

139 In Paul Fregosi, *Jihad in the West* (Amherst, N.Y., 1998), 346.

Chapter 4: The Road to Nowhere

1 *The European Dream*, 384.

2 A recent analysis of these same problems can be found in Walter Lacqueur, *The Last Days of Europe* (New York, 2007).

Notes

3 In *The Economist* (27 May 2006), 22.

4 *The New York Times* (26 March 2007); see also the essay by Conrad Black, "Europe's Dream Disturbed," *The National Interest* (Fall, 2005); Theodore Dalrymple, "Is 'Old Europe' Doomed?" *Cato Unbound* (6 February 2006), available at http://www.cato-unbound.org/2006/02/06/theodore-dalrymple/is-old-europe-doomed/.

5 In *The New York Times* (25 March 2007).

6 For a defense of the nation state, see Pierre Manent's essay *A World Beyond Politics*, trans. Marc Le Pain (2001; Princeton, 2006).

7 In *In the Name of Humanity*, trans. Judith Friedlander (1996; New York, 2000), 103.

8 Philip Jenkins has recently argued that the reports of European Christianity's death are exaggerated, as are fears of Muslim immigrant radicalism and fecundity. *In God's Continent* (Oxford and New York, 2007).

9 Tony Judt, *Postwar*, 728.

10 See the remarks by Jed Babbin, *Inside the Asylum* (Washington, D.C., 2004), 119-38; Lieber, *The American Era*, 82–88.

11 "The Modern Dilemma," in *Christianity and European Culture*, 129.

INDEX

INDEX

INDEX

INDEX

INDEX

INDEX

INDEX

DESIGN & COMPOSITION BY CARL W. SCARBROUGH